Zen Buddhism

About the Authors

Professor L.P. Singh spent about two decades as a mendicant in search of truth and salvation. He was awarded D. Litt. Degree from Ranchi University, Ranchi in 1972. He retired as a professor of Philosophy from Magadh University, Bodh Gaya in January 1996 and in February of the same year he became Senior Fellow of the Indian Council of Philosophical Research, Government of India for three years. In 2000 A.D. Professor Singh was awarded Fellowship of Indian Institute of Advanced Studies, Shimla for three years. He became a visiting Research Professor in 2004 at the Catholic University of America, Washington D.C. He was also awarded Indo-French Cultural Fellowship in 1994. During his sojourn at Paris, he delivered lectures at the Department of Philosophy, Soubourn University IV, Paris. He also addressed the students and staff members of Nihon and Toyo University, Tokyo in 2006. He delivered a special lecture at the Faculty of Humanities and Social Sciences, Khon Kaen University, Thailand in 2013. He presented several papers at the National and International Conferences and Seminars such World Philosophical Congress 1975, International Congress of Orientalists, Mexico City 1976, First Sanskrit Symposia, Mexico City 1982, World Sanskrit Congress, Lieden, Holland, International Conferences at East China Normal University, Shanghai, Xiaotong University, Xi'an in December 2013. He also presented papers at the School of the Social Sciences and the Humanities, East China Normal University and at the School of Social Sciences, Shanghai University, Shanghai, China in 2014. He chaired many International sessions. Twenty one Research Scholars worked under his supervision and were awarded Ph.D. degrees. He has written many books of high academic value, published several papers at the National and International proceedings and Journals of high academic repute. Prof. Singh is a distinguished professor of philosophy and a social activist.

B.M. Sirisena is a great Buddhist scholar and dedicated monk. His religious name is Ven. Dhammika. He did his Ph.D. from Magadh University, Bodh-Gaya under Professor L.P. Singh. He became an english teacher in Japan.

Zen Buddhism

L.P. Singh
B.M. Sirisena

CONCEPT PUBLISHING COMPANY PVT. LTD.
NEW DELHI-110059

ISBN-13: 978-93-5125-288-7

First Published 2018

Published and Printed by

Concept Since 1974

Concept Publishing Company Pvt. Ltd.
A/15-16, Commercial Block, Mohan Garden,
New Delhi-110059 (INDIA)
T : +91 11 25351460, +91 1125351794
E : publishing@conceptpub.com, *W* : www.conceptpub.com

Cataloging in Publication Data--Courtesy: D.K. Agencies (P) Ltd. <docinfo@dkagencies.com>

Singh, Lalan Prasad, 1936- author.
Zen Buddhism / L.P. Singh, B.M. Sirisena.
pages cm
Includes bibliographical references and index.
ISBN 9789351252887

1. Zen Buddhism. 2. Zen Buddhism—Relations. I. Sirisena, B. M., author. II. Title.

LCC BQ9265.4.S56 2018 DDC 294.3927 23

To

My Loving Student

Ven. Dhammika

Preface

Zen Buddhism is a mysticism. It is an esoteric technique to rid the man from the snares of false subjectivities and to take him to the enlightenment (*Satori*). Zen is not a philosophy. It is not a religion. It is a spirituality. It is a pathless path. Zen is a song of silence. Zen is a happy and harmonious blending of science and spirituality.

Zen Buddhism reveals the inner most dimension of our being and existence. The real being is Buddha–nature (*Bodhi-Chitta*). It is a *Satori*. *Satori* is pathless. The quantum question which was raised by Socrates in 3rd century B.C. in form of *Know Thy Self* is being repeated again today by Nobel laureate scientists like Einstein, Heisenberg, Erwin Schrodinger and other in all most in the same linguistic and philosophical form "what we are". "*Where from we have come*". *This is the question.*

Zen's answer this quantum question is "We are all awakened being" "We are all Buddhas". All the mystical schools and traditions have revealed this truth by their seers and saints. God of mysticism is not a person, it is a principle. God is a myth and metaphor.

My endeavor is to bring to light the fundamental truth that has been revealed by Zen masters. Inspite of the fact that we are all awakened being we are still living in the dark night of soul in the Plato's cave. Zen is a discipline which would take us out from the darkness of Plato's cave to the divine light of truth and Satori.

The co-author venerable Dhammika (S.R. Sirisena) was my student. He was my loving student and a dedicated monk. He is very much lodged in my memory and affection.

This edition of Zen Buddhism has been revised and I have added a new chapter as Prologue. I express my deep gratitude to Shri U.P. Singh for his constant guidance and encouragement in the completion of the revised edition. I would express my profound gratitude to Shri Kamal Morarka for his enormous help in my personal and academic pursuits. My grandchildren Kishu , Rishi, Anirvan, Shivam, Janu, Sanu, Misti, Aalia, Rakshu and Mikku are the greatest source of my inspiration and happiness. I put on record my love and blessings to Bantu, Goru, Bittu, Raja, Kavita, Chiyako, Priya, Naina, Manju and Julie for their loving care without which I would not have been able to do anything in my life after the sudden demise of my wife Ahilya in 1995. I express my thanks to Shri Ashok Kumar Mittal, Managing Director of the Concept Publishing Company (P.) Ltd., for taking publication of this book. Ashok is a part of my family and hence I need not to say anything in form of expressing my gratitude in a formal way. Last but not the least I am thankful to Shri Sandeep Jha and Shri V.K. Gupta for their immense help in the completion of this manuscript.

14-08-2017
Janmashtami
New Delhi

Professor L.P. Singh

Contents

CHAPTER 1
Prologue

We are all in quest for our true identity and destiny. In search of ultimate reality and *summon bonum* of life, the Śiva, the Buddha and the Lao Tzu expounded intuitional science, mysticism and philosophical schools known as Hinduism, Buddhism and Taoism. Mysticism forms the basis of all religions and provides sound metaphysical foundation for science and spirituality. Hinduism, Buddhism and Taoism attained the pinnacle of spiritual glory and profound philosophical sublimity in *Advaitism* (non-dualism). The Hindu seers, Buddhist patriarchs and Taoist experienced the existential quest for human identity and destiny which is called enlightenment. Sixth century B.C. is known in world history as an era of renaissance. The Buddha, the Lao Tzu and Parmenides regenerated for the first time mankind spiritually and intellectually.

With the evolution of *Homo sapiens* man became gradually conscious of self and nature and he started reflecting on the quantum question "Who am I", "where from have we come?" Question which have been reiterated by Erwin Schrodinger, "I know not whence I came not whither I go nor who I am. This is my situation as yours, every single one of you."[1]

After getting enlightenment under *Bodhi* tree at Bodhgaya, the Buddha started reflecting on the nature and the signification of *Satori*, which resulted into the birth of a new school of philosophy and religion known as Buddhism. Siddhārtha became Buddha, the enlightened one. He spent seven weeks at and around *Bodhi* tree and ultimately resolved to decimate his sublime and profound mystic experience and left for Sāranātha where he delivered his first sermon known as *Dharmacakra Parivartana sūtra*. His teachings were pregnant with deep and profound metaphysical and spiritual imports which have been interpreted by different historians and Buddhist patriarchs at the different periods of history which gave the birth of a different schools and sects of Buddhism. However, the fundamental teaching of the Buddha veers around *Nirvāṇa*. Buddhism is a philosophy of compassion and enlightenment. It is a mystic discipline for the attainment of enlightenment.

Zen Buddhism is an ontological mysticism. *Bodhidharma* is considered as the founder of this mystic school of Buddhism. He occupies the same place of veneration in the history of Buddhism as that of Nāgārjuna and Vasuvandhu, the founder of *Mādhyamikā* and *Yogācarya* respectively. *Bodhidharma* was a prince of a small kingdom of South India. He was initiated into Buddhism by the great Buddhist teacher Prajñatara. Like Lao Tzu who left China after painful experience of decadence of Chaou dynasty, *Bodhidharma* also left India after getting saddened by the decline of Buddhism in India, where it was originated and left for China. It is stated that he completed his journey in three years and finally landed on the Southern shore of China in 520 AD. He settled at Shaolin monastery on Mount Shongshan. He started practising meditation facing the cliff of the mountain in front of the monastery. The place became known in history as wall-gazing hermitage. People started addressing him as Biguan (the wall gazing monk). Buddhism has already taken root in China. The Shaolin monastery became famous for the centre of martial arts also.

Bodhidharma's visit to China and founding the Zen school of Buddhism has been recorded by many Chinese historians. Richard Bryan McDaniel writes, "Evidence of a historical basis to the story of *Bodhidharma* is found in a document written by an official named Yang Xuanzhi in 547. He recorded that when he visited the temple of Yongning in Luoyang, he came upon an elderly Indian monk named *Bodhidharma* who claimed to be over a hundred years old. Yang noted that the monk expressed great admiration for the beauties of the shrines and other buildings he found in China".[2]

There is a lot of narrations about *Bodhidharma's* visit to China. According to one account *Bodhidharma* visited Luoyang, the capital city of the Liang dynasty founded by emperor Wou. Wou had become a devoted Buddhist and started decimation of Buddhist thoughts through the publication of Buddhist scriptures and establishing monasteries and nunneries. When emperor came to know about the presence of *Bodhidharma* coming from the land of Buddha, he expressed his desire to pay respect to this holy man. When he met

Bodhidharma he enquired about the merit he had accumulated by spreading the Buddhism in his capital. *Bodhidharma's* reply was very straight forward and he said, "No merit you have earned." King was very much disappointed to hear this answer. *Bodhidharma* explained the cause of not earning any merits. He stated that any action done by impure motives does not earn any merit. According to Buddhism motivation is very important. He explained to the emperor that the basic teachings of Buddhism is the ultimate reality of emptiness. Then emperor asked, what does it mean? *Bodhidharma's* reply to this was mystical, "I do not know". This explains the indescribable nature of the ultimate reality (emptiness).

> Those who know do not say
> Those who say do not know
> Close the senses,
> shut the doors;
> blunt the sharpness,
> resolve the complications;
> harmonize the light,
> assimilate to the world.
> This is called mysterious sameness.
> it cannot be made familiar,
> yet cannot be estranged;
> it cannot be profited,
> yet cannot be harmed;
> it cannot be valued,
> yet cannot be demeaned.
> therefore it is precious for the world."[3]

There is a great similarity between Zen Buddhist teachings and Taoism. Only the enlightened one know and understand the unity and the wholeness of all things. In the enlightened one the dualism of the subjective self and the objective self is mingled and transformed into the wholeness and unity of the existence and being.

This has been the problem before all the mystics who have expressed their experiences which are inexpressible. Even a modern philosopher like Ludwig Wittgenstein had to make distinction between 'sayable' and 'unsayable'. There is a reality which cannot be expressed in any language and this is why all the mystics have taken help of expressing those mystic experiences through myths, parables and allegories and Lao Tzu is not an exception to this rule. Taoism is a purely metaphysical and ontological mysticism. It is rooted in mysticism. J. Krishna Murthy says, "Truth is pathless". This pathless path is mysticism. Okakuro-Kakuzo writes, "The Tao is the passage rather than the path. It is the spirit of cosmic change – the eternal growth which returns upon itself to produce new forms. It recoils upon itself like the dragon, the beloved symbol of the Taoists.

It folds and unfolds as to the clouds. The Tao may be spoken as the Great Transition. Subjectively, it is the Mood of the Universe. It is the principle of all energy, yet energy it is not, but merely one of its manifestations. It is the eternal principle of all life, but no life can express it, and all bodies, all material forms, are but its changing and momentary raiment. Sometimes it called "The Mother of all Things" the primordial creative cause, the self-existent source, the unconditioned by which all things are conditioned, for although it does not create, it is the source of all creation. The animating principle of the universe; it is "the unchanging principle which supports the shifting multiplicity."[4]

There is another story related with *Bodhidharma*. A learned Confucian teacher Ji called upon *Bodhidharma* at his hermitage on Mount Shaoshi to seek his help and blessing to get rid from the philosophical entanglement. He was not granted audience immediately, but he was very sincerely waiting outside his monastery, spending many days and nights and when he was covered upto his knees with snow one morning he was given permission to see him. *Bodhidharma* enquired what you are seeking. He said, your spiritual teaching. Ji stated, "My mind is not at peace". *Bodhidharma* said, "Show your mind, I will pacify it". Ji stated that, he had tried through sitting meditations and going through the classical scriptures of Confucianism, but he could not succeed in quieting the mind. *Bodhidharma* touched him and he was enlightened. In the mystic traditions, it is known as *śaktipata* (transmission of light). This could be done only by enlightened *Yogi*. There is a famous story about Vivekananda. When he met Swami Ramakrishna Paramahansa he was touched by Paramahansa. Vivekananda's dormant divinity was awakened. Lord Śiva is the founding father of this esoteric technique of *śaktipata*. It is still alive in the mystic tradition of awakening the dormant divinity in the form of serpent power (*Kuṇḍalinī śakti*) from *guru* to *śiṣya* (disciple). *Śaktipata* by Swami Ramakrishna transformed Narendra Dutta into Vivekananda. The same esoteric technique has been used by Zen masters in awakening the dormant divinity resulting into the attainment of *satori*. Ramakrishna Paramahansa through *śaktipata,* transmitted the mystic experiences and Vivekananda had the realization that the ultimate reality is transcendentality, And he realized the transitory nature of the phenomenal world. *Bodhidharma* came to the same experiential spiritual understanding that the ultimate reality is *Bodhicitta* which was not different from that of all existence.

The modern quantum mechanics is also coming to the same truth. This problem was raised by British philosopher David Hume (1711-1776) that the relation between the cause and effect cannot be explained. He enunciated, what we observe is not the relation between cause and effect but the regular succession which led to the physicist like Ernest Mach to make a very bold statement that classical science does not guarantee any explanation of causation. Erwin Schrodinger observes, "The habit of everyday language deceives us and seems to require whenever we hear the word 'shape' or 'form' pronounced, that it must be the shape or form of something, that a material substratum is required to take on a shape. Scientifically this habit goes back to Aristotle, his *cause materialis* and *causa formalis*. But, when you come to the ultimate particles constituting matter, there seems to be no point in thinking of them again as consisting of some material.

They are as it were, pure shape, nothing but shape; what turns-up again-and-again in successive observations is this shape, not an individual speck of material".[5]

Schrödinger's concept of form is closer to Buddhist suchness (*Tathata*). The Buddhist metaphysics is based on the Nāgārjuna's doctrine of emptiness. According to this doctrine the essential nature of all existence and being is emptiness. It is the *elan vita* and the quintessential nature and source of all reality and it is the essence of all forms and beings.

According to D.T. Suzuki *Avataṁsaka* is the quintessence of Buddhism. He writes, "As to the *Avataṁsaka*, it is really the consummation of the Buddhist thought, Buddhist sentiment, and Buddhist experience. To my mind, no religious literature in the world can ever approach the grandeur of conception, the depth of feeling, and the gigantic scale of composition as attained in this *sūtra*. It is the eternal foundation of life from which no religious mind will turn back athirst or only partially satisfied."[6]

D.T. Suzuki considers *Prajñā* (transcendental wisdom) and *karuṇā* (compassion) as the two pillars of Buddhism. *Prajñā*, the enlightened wisdom and *karuṇā* are the two inalienable part of the Buddhist reality. The sublimity and the profundity of concepts of *Prajñā* (wisdom) and *karuṇā* (compassion) originated in the ideal of *Bodhisattva* which has become the iconic symbol of Mahāyāna Buddhism. According to this tradition *Bodhisattva* is a person who have qualified for attainment of enlightenment and become the Buddha he refuses to attain *Nirvāṇa* for himself unless everybody would before him attains *Nirvāṇa*. Buddhism is a spiritual humanism based on ontological mysticism. Fritjof Capra writes, "The central theme of the *Avataṁsaka* is the unity and the interrelation of all things and events; a conception which is not only the very essence of the Eastern world-view, but also one of the basic elements of the world-view emerging from modern physics. It will therefore be seen that the *Avataṁsaka Sūtra*, this ancient religious text, offers the most striking parallels to the models and theories of modern physics."[7]

Nāgārjuna is credited with bringing the Copernicus revolution in Indian philosophy. A new phase of philosophical thinking and speculation started with Mādhyamikā. Dialectic became a spiritual movement. Dialectic is a process to overcome the universal conflict afflicted by the antinomical character of reason. Nāgārjuna succeeded in overcoming the inherent conflict in reason by refuting both the opposites. According to Nāgārjuna real is spiritual and transcendental. According to Nāgārjuna dialectic is mystical experience which takes man beyond the possibility of pain and pleasure. It is the highest end of our spiritual pursuits. It is salvation (*Nirvāṇa*).

T.R.V. Murti writes, "The dialectic as *Prajñāpāramitā* is identified with the *tathāgata* (*dharmakāya*) — the Ens perfectissimum, which all beings are in essence and which they attain by spiritual discipline. Religion is the mystic pull of the Transcendent (the Ideal) on the actual. The dialectic consummates the union of all beings with the perfect Being (*Buddha-kāya*). In Kant, the Critique silences theoretic (Pure) Reason; its function is thus merely negative. It is the Practical Reason that alone guarantees to Kant his ideals, God, freedom and immortality. There is thus the severance of the intellectual form the ethical and the religious.

The *Mādhyamikā* Dialectic as negation of thought is intuition of the Absolute as the rooting out of passions it is Freedom (*Nirvāṇa*);

and it is perfection as union with the Perfect Being."[8] The Buddhist dialectic culminates in mystical ontology. The terms *Śūnya* and *Śūnyatā* connotes both the relativity and the absolute. The absolute (emptiness) is *Śūnya* as it is beyond the conceptual distinctions of existence and non-existence. It is a state of absolute freedom from all kinds of false subjectivity. Philosophy becomes a pursuit of not knowledge but quest for *Prajñāpāramitā* (perfection).

In *Kashmir Śaivism* this mystic technique is known as *Anupāya*. *Anupāya* is sudden and spontaneous experience of *satori* without any special practice. *Śiva sūtra*, the canonical literature of *Kashmir Śaivism* explains this esoteric technique through which self realisation is attained without any practise of *yoga*. Abhinava Gupta, the great authority and the author of *Tantrāloka* talks very high of this esoteric technique of *Anupāya*. He writes—

उपायजालं न शिवं प्रकाशयेद्
घटेन किं भाति सहस्रदीधितिः ।
विवेचयन्नित्थमुदारदर्शनः
स्वयंप्रकाशं शिवमाविशेत्क्षणात् ।।

Self-realization is not possible without the grace and *Śaktipāda*. Innumerable practice of *Yoga* cannot reveal Śiva (cosmic consciousness). Can zar reveal the sun. Thus with the *Anupāya* technique one could get the whole vision of the transcendentality (*Śiva*) which is self-luminous. This state of *satori* is beyond the reach of senses and language. It could not be formulated in linguistic form. Abhinava Gupta explains this mystic experience in his book as the first and the last freedom in the same metaphor. He coined a word to explain this inexplicable experience of transcendentality as *unmeṣa*. *Unmeṣa* means the complete liberation from the trammels of *māyā* (nascence). It is a state of *nirvāṇa* (self-realization). The seventh verse of *Śiva Sūtra*,

जाग्रत्स्वप्नसुषुप्तभेदे तुर्याभोगसंभवः ।। 7 ।।

In the seventh verse it has been explained that this is a state of consciousness which is a witnessing entity. Mircea Eliade talks very high of this Indian contribution – He writes "It is impossible, for example, to disregard one of India's greatest discoveries: that of consciousness as witness, of consciousness freed from its psycho-physiological structures and their temporal conditioning, the consciousness of the 'liberated' man, of him, that is, who has succeeded in emancipating himself from temporarily and thereafter knows the true, inexpressible freedom. The conquest of his absolute freedom, of perfect spontaneity, is the goal of all Indian philosophies and mystical techniques; but it is above all through *Yoga*, through one of the many forms of *Yoga*, that India has held that it can be assured."[9]

There are four stages of consciousness, *Jāgrata* (waking state), *svapna* (the state of dream), *suṣupti* (state of deep sleep), *tūrya* (state of consciousness which is the state of *samādhi*). J. Krishna Murty calls it the state of choice-less awareness. Jaidev Singh writes, "*Anupāya* is, really speaking, *Sāmbhava yoga* itself in its highest maturity

स (शाम्भवोपायः) एव परां काष्ठां प्राप्तश्चानुपाय इत्युच्यते।

The *Sāmbhava Upāya* itself, in its highest maturity is known as *Anupāya*. "Later on, the word *Sahasa* was employed by Vatulanātha of Kashmir to express the idea of *Sāmbhava yoga* and *Anupāya*. The word *Sahasa* means sudden, unexpected happening. It beautifully expresses the idea of sudden spontaneous flash of the Experience of the Divine Self. The ultimate aim of both *Sāṁkhya-yoga* and *Vedānta* is *mukti* (liberation). By *mukti*, both of them understand *Kaivalya*, perfect isolation of Soleness, the only difference being that *Sāṁkhya-yoga* aims at isolation from *Prakṛti* while *Vedānta* aims at isolation from *Māyā*."[10]

During Tang dynasty a disciple asked from the Zen master, "What is great *nirvāṇa*?" The Zen master replied, "Not to commit oneself to the *karma* of birth and death is *nirvāṇa*". The disciple enquired "What then is the *karma* of birth and death?" The monk replied, "Desire to get *nirvāṇa* is the *karma* of birth and death". The Zen master's reply does not speak of the Procrustean logical narration. Zen does not believe in intellectualization of transcendental reality. Zen believed that the enlightenment could be attained only when it is not desired. To desire is to create a metempsychosis and so long someone is desiring and thereby creating a new *karma*, *nirvāṇa* is always beyond the reach.

According to *Mahāyāna* ultimate reality is emptiness which is indescribable. The *Visuddhi Magga* says, "As to void, singlefold, and so on: firstly as to void: in the ultimate sense all the truths should be understood as void because of the absence of (i) any experience, (ii) any doer, (iii) anyone who is extinguished, and (iv) any goer. Hence this is said:

> For there is suffering, but none who suffers;
> Doing exists although there is no doer;
> Extinction is but no extinguished person;
> Although there is a path, there is no goer.[11]

There is a great similarity between the Zen masters formulation of desirelessness as necessary conditions for the attainment of enlightenment and St. Paul's Epistle to Corinthians as stated below –

And they that weep, as though they wept not; and they that rejoice, as though they rejoiced not; and they that buy, as though they possessed not; and they that use this world, as not abusing it (I Cor. 7: 30). The Taoist concept of Wu-Wei is the Zen technique of desirelessness.

Taoism put emphasis for the practice of asceticism. Life of indulgence leads to degeneration of our life. Passions and the cravings bring degeneration of our vitality and loss of soul. The man who lives a life of indulgence cannot experience spirituality and mystical union with the Tao. Such man loses the faculty of listening to the inner sounds of silence and inner light of spirituality. He no longer enjoys the divine bliss of "savor of the Tao".

Wu-wei is one of the root concepts of Taoism. Wu-wei is translated into 'No-Activity'. The doctrine of no-activity has again been used in many senses. No-activity stands for living a natural life. Living a natural life means living a life according to the Te. The Te distinguishes between natural and unnatural actions.

To live a natural life is the goal of the Indian *Yogis* also. Normally, people do not live according to the law of nature and this creates the ripples in the mind in form of cravings and desires. The whole purpose of *Yoga* is to rid one-self from the cravings and mundane desires. This is known in *Patañjala Yoga* as *Citta* (tendency). To overcome and root out all the cravings is the purpose and the goal of *Yoga Sādhanā*. And when a practicner through the practise of *Yoga* root out all the tendencies and cravings he attains mystic Trance (*Samādhi*). It is called *Sahaja Samādhi* (natural state of being an existence).Tao is considered as maternal principle. The concept of mother, female, mystical womb is equated with the Tao and emptiness. This emptiness is equated with the concept of Wu.

Max Kaltenmark writes, "We have several times already come across the expression wu-wei: 'without doing,' 'absence of action.' Wu is not the same as nothingness, and Wu-wei is not an ideal of absolute inaction; on the contrary, it is particularly efficacious attitude since it makes all doing possible."[12]

Inactivity does not mean laziness. In Taoism, this concept has been used in the context of the mysticism. In the state of enlightenment there is no activity. The state of the Tao or the Brahman of Hinduism is a state of spiritual sublimity and in that state of enlightenment and *Nirvāṇa* there is a complete absence of any activity because individuality is merged in the Tao. When there is no individuality there can be no activity. When a man enters into the mystic union with reality he loses his individuality. Action is related to individuality and in the state of *Nirvāṇa* and enlightenment the world becomes unreal and illusion from the transcendental perspective. So, the Taoism here speaks about the inactivity or no-action from the perspective of ontological mysticism. In the Western culture there is complete absence of the concept of enlightenment and *Nirvāṇa*. This is why the western mind has difficulty in understanding the mystical and the metaphysical import of the concept of the Wu-wei.

Wu-wei figures three times in the first seven chapters of the Chuang Chou. Wu-wei means "by its side you wander in non-action: under it you may sleep in happiness", "Tao has reality and evidence, but no action and form"; "They stroll beyond the dirty world and wander in the realm of inaction". This speaks of the Taoist non-partition in the mundane activities. It means only by inner renunciation and withdrawal from the worldly activities one can enter into the world of the Tao. Both the Lao Tzu and Chuang Chou adherence to Wu-wei means no activity springing from the absence of worldly cravings and desires. This is kernel of Taoism, Hinduism and Buddhism. Unless one roots out all his cravings and mundane desires one cannot attain mystic union with cosmic consciousness which is called the mother in all the oriental canonical literatures. The concept mother has figuratively used as a progenitor and womb of cosmos.

In Taoism emptiness expressed as Wu. The Wu is explained as nothingness and non-activity. It would be wrong to indentify the Wu with the void. In Taoism the void is pregnant with all potentiality. The emptiness has been enumerated in Tao Te Ching in the following verse.

16. Attain the Climax of Emptiness
Attain the climax of emptiness,
preserve the utmost quiet:
as myriad things act in concert,
I thereby observe the return.
Things flourish,
then each returns to its root.

Returning to the root is called stillness:

stillness is called return to Life,
return to Life is called the constant;
knowing the constant is called enlightenment.
Acts at random, in ignorance of the constant, bode ill.
Knowing the constant gives perspective;
this perspective is impartial.
Impartiality is the higher nobility;
the highest nobility is divine,
and the divine is the Way.
This Way is everlasting,
not endangered by physical death.[13]

Both Zen and Taoism are related to our everyday life itself. Neither Tao nor Zen could be predicated. To define Tao is not a Tao. To explain Zen is not a Zen. Zen is a discipline in enlightenment. Zen is an esoteric discipline in *satori*. D.T. Suzuki writes, "Zen is discipline in enlightenment. Enlightenment means emancipation. And emancipation is no less than freedom.

We talk very much these days about all kinds of freedom, political, economic and otherwise, but these freedoms are not at all real. As long as they are on the plane of relativity, the freedom or liberties we glibly talk about are far from being such. The real freedom is the outcome of enlightenment. When a man realises this, in whatever, situation he may find himself he is always free in his inner life, for that pursues its own line of action. Zen is the religion of *jiyu* (*tzu-yu*), "self-reliance" and *jizai* (*tzu-tsai*), self-being."[14]

According to Buddhism and Hinduism metaphysics is transformed into soteriological virtue. Unless the knowledge of reality paves the path for the attainment of enlightenment it does not have any importance. The *Vidyā*, the *Jñāna* and *Prajñā* stand for soteriological purpose. Vācaspati Miśra while commenting on Ishvarakṛṇṣa writes, "In this world, the audience listens only to the preacher who sets forth facts whose knowledge is necessary and desired. To those who set forth doctrines that no one desires, no one attends, as comes to pass with fools or with men of the herd, who are good in their practical affairs but ignorant of the sciences and arts."[15]

The same author, in his commentary on the *Vedānta-sūtra-bhāṣya*, specifies the necessary knowledge: "No lucid person desires to know what is devoid of all certainty or what is of no use... or of no importance."[16]

The Western Civilization is dominated by historicity and temporality of human existence. Max Weber considered that man is culturally structured. According to some it is environment that plays an important role in conditioning the man behaviour. Man is a conditioned being. The Buddhist and Hinduism hold a different view all together. According to Buddhism man is conditioned by his or her past *karma* (*prārabdha*). The ontological cause is the ignorance. It does not mean that every kind of ignorance is the cause of bondage. The ignorance of the real nature of the consciousness (*ātman or Śūnyatā*) that creates psycho-mental experience is bondage. Every action has equal and opposite reaction. Reaction in its potentiality is called *prārabdha*. To de-condition himself from the past *karma* has been central objective of Indian culture and civilization. Buddhism and Hinduism are a trans-historical and a-temporal technique to de-condition himself and get enlightenment. According to both Buddhism and Hinduism man is a hibernated cosmic being. Reality is cosmic consciousness. In Buddhism it is called *Śūnyatā* and in Hinduism it is called Brahman. The cosmic consciousness is the witnessing force. The meditational technique has been employed both in Buddhism and Hinduism to de-condition himself and enter into the state of non-duality and to go beyond the time, causation and creation. Philosophers and scientists have been pondering on truth and reality since time immemorial. Western Civilization is proud of its monumental achievements in natural science and technology.

Eastern civilization especially that of India have made profound contribution in the form of intuitional science and mysticism. The most profound ontological doctrine is considered to be the *Mādhyamikā* which claims *Śūnyatā* to be an intrinsic nature, to be in ultimate mode of existence of phenomenon.

One can experience *Śūnyatā* only when the mind is liberated from all kinds of reification. However, Buddhist *Tantra* is aware of the futility of speculative philosophy and hence it recommends the practice of esotericism to experience the enlightenment in which essence and existence become identical. Western philosophy has acknowledged that Zen Buddhism has made enormous discoveries and achievements in terms of intuitional science and mysticism which have a sound metaphysical, epistemological and soteriological basis.

Mind cannot maintain its existence without objectivity. Mind is a state in the process of evolution. It is a stage in the process of motion. Every motion is an alternated phase of pause and speed. Every movement is pulsative. In the stage of pause it gains momentum which it has to express. Mind resorts to certain inter and intra-ectoplasmic occupations to express itself. These occupations and conations of mind are known as tendencies or *vṛttis*. These tendencies or *vṛttis* are the ways of expression of mind. In psychology they are called instincts. Pineal and pituitary glands are two important and the most vital glands, the rest are all called subsidiary glands. *Vṛttis* are the psychic objectives of mind. They are the colours and contours of the mental process.

The *Satori* is unity of wisdom and the bliss. Zen Buddhism entered into the consciousness of the West by formulating the mystic technique of de-conditioning the human being. Man is not a temporal and historical being but he is a *Buddha*-nature. He is a cosmic consciousness.

The Buddha after attainment of *nirvāṇa* under *Bodhi* tree at Bodhgaya reflected on the nature and significance of *nirvāṇa* which resulted into a birth of a new school of philosophy known as Buddhism. Zen Buddhism is the sublime and profound form of spirituality and mysticism. It presents the highest form of *Advaita* (non-dual). The most profound ontological doctrine is considered to be *Mādhyamikā* which claims *Śūnyatā* to be the intrinsic nature, to be the ultimate mode of being and existence. One can experience *Śūnyatā* only when the mind is liberated from all kinds of mental reification. Zen Buddhism is aware of the futility of speculative metaphysics and hence it puts emphasis on the practice of *dhyāna* for the realization of *satori*. In this intuitive experience essence and existence, knowledge and the bliss become identical. The search of the ultimate reality and freedom has been the quint essential teachings of Hinduism and Buddhism. The realization of consciousness in its pure form and transcendentality is the central objective of Buddhism and Hinduism. The *Upaniṣad* and *Buddhist sūtras* state that all sentient beings are *ātman* or *Buddha*-nature but we do not have the realization of our real nature of being and existence. This is a big paradoxical problem that haunts before the seeker of enlightenment.

Buddha has also stated that all beings are inherently liberated, then why the Buddha has to undergo through the long years of quest for salvation. Why *Bodhidharma* had to spend nine years at the Shaolin monastery in China to meditation. The Vedantic explanation is that we have erroneously identified ourselves with non-self and this is called bondage. According to Buddhism one can experience *Buddha* nature when mind is liberated from all kinds of mental reifications and to get the mental reification one will have to *dhyāna* (meditation). This will take one from the snares of false subjectivity and take him to the state of *satori*. To get answer to this vexed philosophical problem, the great Japanese Zen Master, Dogan visited Kenninji Temple to meet Eisai. Dogan asked to the master, "The scriptures say, that we all have the *Buddha*-nature. Why is it that the enlightened masters have to practice *dhyāna* to attain this state of choice-less awareness?" Eisai's answer is very short but meaningful. No Buddha is conscious of having *Buddha*-nature, only the shallow are aware of it."

Dajian Huineng is one of the greatest Zen masters coming from a very poor family of Southern China. His life is recorded in the Platform *Sūtra* of the Sixth Patriarch. He was illiterate and without any respectful background. When Huineng was only three years old, he lost his father and the burden of the family came upon him. He lived in abject poverty. When he was passing through a mountain area he heard somebody reciting the diamond *sūtra*. He enquired from the man who was reciting the diamond sutra and came to know that he learnt it from the Buddhist master Hongren who was living at East Mountain monastery. He decided to meet the Hongren, the fifth patriarch. He left his village handing over his mother in the care of co-villager. When he met the fifth patriarch he expressed his desire to attain Buddhahood. The master put him to test by asking how it is possible for someone like you to attain enlightenment and you are coming from Southern part of China which are inhabited by barbarians and who do not have *Buddha* nature. Huineng answered that, the *Buddha*-nature does not make any discrimination between the Southerners and the Northerners, the barbarians and the educated person. Hongren, the master was very much impressed by his reply and asked him to stay in the monastery and help in cooking. Once Huineng was very devoted to his work and kept himself engaged in meditation. The master could realize that he is the only one in the whole monastery who have the awareness and the commitment for enlightenment. Hongren after sometime conveyed in the meeting of all his disciples his desire to retire. The search for the sixth Patriarch started. Everybody was certain that Shenxiu, the senior most monk would succeed the fifth patriarch. The master asked them to display their knowledge and understanding of Zen and asked them to compose a *gāthā*. Shenxiu inscribed the *gāthā*, one of the walls of the monastery. He stated,

> The body is like the *Buddha*-tree,
> the mind a stand with a mirror bright.
> Take care to wipe it clean,
> and donot let dust or dirt alight!

Huineng was hulling rice when he heard about this *gāthā*. He inquired from the monk about the *gāthā*. The monk disdainfully stated that for you, the Southern Barbarians it is beyond your reach and understanding. Huineng said, I have also composed a *gāthā*, could you inscribe it on the wall for me? as he was illiterate. His *gāthā* is as follows –

> The body is not tree,
> nor the mind a mirror bright.
> Since from the beginning not a thing exists,
> where can dirt and dust alight?

Huineng's *gāthā* speaks of the profundity and the sublimity of Zen teachings, whereas Shenxiu *gāthā* lacks the real understanding and the knowledge of Zen teachings. Hongren selected him, the sixth patriarch and asked him to meet at midnight and he handed over *Bodhidharma's* bowl and robe to Huineng. The fifth patriarch was worried that the other senior disciples and the monks would not accept him as his successor and would be after his blood and hence he asked him to leave the monastery immediately. One of the senior monk thought that the barbarians had taken away the sacred relics of the first patriarch and went away. The senior monks started hunting him, ultimately one monk named Ming spotted Huineng at mountain pass. Huineng kept the robe and the bowl on the rock and waited for Ming to take the possession of it. Ming tried his level best to take possession of the sacred robe but he could not succeed because he failed in lifting the robes and the bowls of the first patriarch. Then Ming realised that Huineng was rightful successor of the fifth patriarch. This is the narration of one of the greatest patriarch who settled at Baolin Monastery.

Richard Bryan McDaniel writes, "After this, Huineng established himself at the Baolin Monastery in the mountains of the South, and here it is said thousands of people came seeking to become his disciples. His fame spread as far as the capital, where the emperor invited him to move, but Huineng declined the invitation as his master, Hongren, had done before him. Meanwhile, in the north, Hongren's chief monk, Shenxiu was gathering his own following."[17]

Meditation has occupied a prominent and important place in all the schools of *Mahāyāna* Buddhism. The importance and over emphasis on meditation as special technique and doctrines with Taoist influence has emerged as Zen sect, generally considered specifically Chinese product.[18]

However *Bodhidharma* introduced a new concept of two entrances and four deeds in the technique of *dhyāna* which enriched the *Mahāyāna* mind, tranquilization. *The Encyclopaedia of Buddhism* says, "the first of the entrances, entrance by reason means (1) to receive the law from a Master and believe that all living things have the same true (Buddha); Nature (2) to meditate on this idea and by having an unshakable faith in it, became one with it, so that the distinction between oneself an others and others as well as between the unenlightened man and the Buddha are eliminated; and (3) not to rely completely on the printed word, but to come naturally to truth and dwell peacefully and contently in it".[19]

The concept of meditation has been examined and interpreted in the different schools of Buddhism differently, but it has been accepted and adhered by all that it is an esoteric technique to get the mind free from all kinds of reification. However, the central objective of all schools of meditation is to integrate the part with whole and this process of esoteric unification *satori* is experienced. This mystic experience has been considered as an act of walking with no path, no walker and no goal. These apparent nonsensical statements contain great spiritual significations.

This mystic technique of meditation is a process of emptying oneself from all kinds of mental dispositions and defilements.

According to Ontological mystic perspective, it is ultimate reality that is one and homogenous being. It is emptiness, it is cosmic consciousness. World and reality are constituted of this. It is beyond the reach of both philosophy and science. Ludwig Wittgenstein, also talks about mysticism. He says, "There are indeed things that cannot be put into words. They make themselves manifest. They are what is mystical. My proposition serve as elucidations in the following way: anyone who understands me eventually recognizes them as non-sensical, when he has used them – as steps – to climb up beyond them. (He must, so to speak, throw away the ladder after he has climbed up it.)

He must transcend these propositions, and then only he will see the world aright. What we cannot speak about we must pass over in silence."[20]

According to Zen Buddhism, neither exact science is really possible nor does any philosophical knowledge comprehend the nature of reality.

Zen monk, Nyogen Senjaki collected 101 Zen stories which depict the important events of life of the Buddha's and some other Zen monks of China and Japan who played an important role in propagating and popularizing the Zen teachings in the West. Later, it was translated by his student in 1939 in English.

These stories are narrations of the important events in the life of Buddha and other ZEN masters of China and Japan. This selection became very famous and it would be called as an introduction to the Zen perspective of mysticism. This book became so popular that it was published by Senjaki and his American disciple which is known as *Mumnkam*. All these narrations of the important events and perspectives of Zen masters was published in a single volume named as Zen Flesh, Zen Bones in 1957 which captivated the seekers of truth and enlightenment in the West.

There is a story about a Zen master named Tanzen of Japan. One of the stories of this monk became the icon of American picture book for children. Story goes like this. Tanzen and his student Ekido were travelling through the rural landscapes of Japan. While they were travelling heavy rain started pouring. A young beautiful lovely girl in her traditional silk attire *kimono* was getting problem in crossing the muddy rivulet. The monk lifted her in his arms and helped her in crossing the muddy water. His student was very much disturbed with the generosity of his teacher. When both of them reached the monastery the student enquired from his masters. "As per the Buddhist ethics monk does not touch and get near the females especially the young and lovely one. Why did you lifted the girl in your arms". The master answered his student's query which speaks of enlightened soul of Tanzen. Master said "I left the girl there, are you still carrying her."

Inspite of the technological and economic development people are very much dissatisfied and would like to return back to the age of tribal dance. The whole Western civilization and culture are suffering from Faustian bargain. The great German historian Spengler has made an scathing attack on the Western culture where the religious and moral function is replaced by hedonism in his monumental work. The Decline of the West. Spengler has stated in this book that Western civilization has become Faustian. Over indulgence in sensuous pleasure is creating disharmony and tension in the world. Schumacher in his famous book The Small is Beautiful has stated that world has enough to satisfy everybody's need but not everybody's greed. The greed of man is leading towards conflict and violence. It is endangering the very survival of mankind. This book is a treatise of Gandhian philosophy.

However, there is a silver lining in the philosophy of Zen Buddhism. There is one very famous Japanese monk Ryokan. He started living far from the madding crowd and helter and shelter of city life to the valley of peace and tranquility.

It is very difficult to abandon the pervasive life of gratification of senses and pleasure and follow the path of enlightenment and spirituality. "However, much the antics of this monk may appeal to our sense of romance, the relevance to life in a modern city is little hard to perceive at first. Where Ryokan lived in the humblest of huts in the hills, most people today live in comfortable houses in congested cities, and where Ryokan spent his days on his begging rounds, helping in the villages, and playing with children, today lives are generally jam packed with work and social commitments. And yet despite the cavernous cultural and historical divide between the life of a nature — loving monk and that of today's city dwellers, there still remains in most of us craving for the simplicity that such life represents".[21]

There is another story about the Zen master of Japan named as a Ryokan. Ryokan was an enlightened Zen monk. Once he was requested by householder to write a special calligraphy which would grant peace and fortune to his family he depicted the character of *shi* (death). There is a great similarity between the narrations of Ryokan with the story of *Mahābhārata*. The story of *Mahābhārata* in philosophical terminology it could be called as Quantum question "What is the greatest wonder in the world." The *Yudhiṣṭhira's* reply speaks of depth and thorough understanding of impermanence of life. *Yudhiṣṭhira's* replied that people experience death taking place everyday but men are not aware that he would also die one day. If the man would understand the signification of death and the impermanence of life he would not indulge in unethical life of greed and violence. While justifying the writing of death calligraphy Ryokan explained that "when people are mindful of death they would not waste time in frivolous activity". Civilization which does not have in depth study and evaluation of depth is incomplete. Death is a celebration of life and life is a celebration of death. Life and death are one in the vast stream of existence.

Hakuin Ekaku is one of the most revered Zen monks of Japan belonging to Rinzai Zen tradition. He exercised so much impact on the Zazen practice that the Rinzai Zen was known as Hakuin Zen. There is a very famous story about him. When he was living in a monastery his neighbour discovered that his young and beautiful daughter has become pregnant. Her father pressed his daughter to name the person who had impregnated her. In the beginning she did not disclose the name of the person. However, when she was tormented by her father she out of fear mentioned the name of Zen monk Hakuin. When the girl gave birth to the child her father has taken that child to the monastery where Hakuin was living. Her father told the monk "This is your child; you take care of the baby".

Hakuin said, "Is that so" Hakuin without any remorse and distress took the care of the child and nurtured the baby to the best of his ability. After a year when Hakuin was begging for food with the baby the consense of the girl was awakened and she admitted to her father that the Zen monk Hakuin was not the real father of the child. The real father of the baby was a young man working at the market with whom she had fallen in love and she became pregnant. The father of the girl went to the monastery and deeply apologized for having discredited Hakuin. Her father said "venerable sir my daughter has consented to marry the young man with whom she had fallen in love and begged him to return back the child. Hakuin said "*Is that so*".

Hakuin was one of the most original thinkers. His following sermon speaks out his profound understanding of Buddhism. "My humble advice to you distinguished persons who study the profound mystery of the *Buddhadharma* is this: Your close examination of yourself must be as urgent as saving your own head were it ablaze: your efforts to penetrate into your own original nature must be as tireless as the pursuit of an indispensable thing: your attitude toward the verbal teachings of the Buddhas and patriarchs must be as hostile as that toward a deadly enemy". Hakuin was a teacher with profound understanding of Zen Buddhism. He encouraged the questioning from his disciples. He stated "underline great doubt there is great *satori* ; where there is thorough questioning there will be thorough going experience of awaking". His koan is still practiced amongst the Zen disciples in Japan and in the West. Some of the poems which are composed stating the mystic signification of Zazen are still chanted in the Zen monasteries throughout the world.

> "From the beginning all beings are Buddha.
> Like water and ice, without water no ice,
> Outside us no Buddhas.
> How near the truth, yet how far we seek,
> Like one in water crying "I thirst"
> Like a child of rich birth
> Wand'ring poor on this earth,
> We endlessly circle the six worlds.
> The cause of our sorrow is ego delusion.
> From dark path to dark path we've wandered in darkness,
> How can we be free the wheel of *saṁsāra*
> (birth and death) ?
> Our thought now being no-thought
> Our dancing and songs are the voice of the *Dharma*.
> How vast is the heaven of boundless *Samādhi*!
> How bright and transparent the moonlight of wisdom!
> What is there outside us, what is there we lack ?
> *Nirvāṇa* is openly shown to our eyes.
> This earth where we stand is the pure lotus land,
> And this very body, the body of Buddha.

In January 1769 Hakuin attained *mahāparinirvāṇa* at the age of 83.

There are great similarities between the Zen Buddhist mystical tradition with other mystical tradition such as the Nāthaism, *Sahajiya* Cult and the Boul of India, and Pythagorean of Greece and Sufism of Iran.

Pythagoreaism and Zen

Pythagorean was founded by Pythagoras in 6th century B.C. who was deeply influenced by mathematics and mysticism. Pythagoras made a great impact on Socrates, Plato and Aristotle. Pythagorean School produced large number of mystical songs which were considered necessary for cleansing the mind and the soul from the passions. This mystical school is a mixture of diatonic, chromatic and enharmonic tunes through which soul is free from irrational passions and desires such as angers egoism and vangians. The arrangements of the melodies are based on the concept of virtue and divinity.

Pythagorean teaching is best on Mathematics and Mysticism. Werner Heisenberg highlighted the contribution of Pythagoras while discussing Atomic Physics with Sommerfeld and Wolfgang he writes Sommerfeld hopes that experiments will help us to find some of the new laws. He believes in numerical links, almost in a kind of number mysticism of the kind the Pythagoreans applied to the harmony of vibrating strings. That's why many of us have called this side of his science "*atomysticism*" though, as far as I can tell, no one has been able to suggest anything better.[22]

Pythagorean Society was an ecstatic society. Pythagorean mystical tradition believes in the doctrine of reincarnation and rebirth like Hinduism and Buddhism. The Pythagorean's believe that relief from the cycle of birth and death would be obtained by mystical practices. Pythagorean religious perspective and life style are rigorous and ascetic like Zen. They also believe in asceticism and the purity of life. Pythagoras is considered as the founding father of Arithmetic which is the Science of numbers. Pythagorean's mathematical idea and concept were developed by Thales, Anaximander, Anaximenes. Teaching of Pythagoreans exercised great influence to Copernicus in formulating his ground breaking theory that it is earth that moves round the sun. This is called heliocentric hypothesis. While summarizing the teaching of Pythagorean Burnett says, "we are stranger in this world, and the body is the tomb of the soul, and yet we must not seek to escape by self-murder for we are chattels of God who is our herdsman, and without his command we have no right to make our escape. In this life, there are three kinds of men, just as there are three sorts of people who come to the Olympic Games. The lowest class is made of those who come to buy and sell, the next above them are those who compete. Best of all, however, are those who come simply to look on. The greatest purification of all is, therefore, disinterested science, and it is the man who devotes himself to that, the true philosopher, who has effectually released himself from the "wheel of birth".[23]

The Pythagorean concept of substance is based on ontological mysticism. Anaximander the great disciple of Pythagoras believed that ultimate reality is "The boundless". He coined the word the *apeiron* for the ultimate boundless reality. According to some scholars the legacy of Pythagoras, Socrates and Plato was claimed by the wisdom tradition of the Hellenized Jews of Alexandria, on the ground that their teachings were derived from those of Moses. Through Alexandria this tradition passed into the medieval culture, with the idea that groups of the same number are related or in sympathy. This idea evidently influenced Hegal in his concept of internal relations. To my mind Pythagoras was a great mystic saint and his philosophy is based on metaphysical and mystical truth like the Buddha, the *Bodhidharma* and other mystical's saints and seers. Pythagorean and Zen spiritual practices are rooted in mysticism. Both these traditions do not believe in formalities and intellectualism. Both these traditions would like to return back to natural state of monism and mysticism by rid the mind from all kinds of false subjectivities. Pythagorean Society and the Zen both believe that by meditation and asceticism alone one can experience the truth and reality.

Sahajiya Cult and Zen

There is a mystical tradition of India known as *Sahajiya* Cult. It is closely related with the Zen Buddhism. There have been Eighty Four *Siddhāchārya* who enriched the philosophical and the mystical practices of *Sahajiya* Culture. The Eighty Four mystic saints of *Chariyapada* emphasized the life of virtue and divinity through which one could attend enlightment. There has been the practice of *Śaktipata* like Zen Buddhism where it is called transmission of light. Mystic tradition is like walking on the razors edge.

The mystic saints of *Sahajiya* cult come from Bengal, Mithila, Odisha and Kamrup. It speaks of the cultural form of Eastern Indians like other mystical schools. *Sahajiya* cult has taken help of myths and metaphors, fables and allegories to explain the truth and reality as truth is unspeakable.

The myths and metaphors are pointer to the greater truth than truth itself. The whole *Chariyapada* literature is written in *Sandhiyā Bhāṣā* (Twilight language). There is a great impact of Tantricism and Vaiṣṇavism in *Chariyapada*.

Lahipa, Lilapa, Virupa, Dombipa, Sabara (*Sabaripa*), Kanari (Āryadeva), Salipa (*Śṛgala-pada*), Tilo-pa (*Tailikapa*), Bhalipa are some of the prominent mystics saints amongst the eighty four *Siddhā Cārya*. *Sahaja* Cult is not a separate and independent school of Tantric Buddhism. It is only another name of *Vajrayāna*. *Sahaja* means straight. It signifies the straight path of Heruka (*kuṇḍalinī*) the awakening of which brings the infinite bliss (*Mahāsukha*). Awakening is possible by the help of *Vajra-Tārā* (another Buddhist name of the *Kuṇḍalinī*) whose path is *Avadhūtikā*. The path of *Avadhūtikā* is straight and not zig-zag likes that of Lalana and Rasana. In Hindu *Tantra*, *Kuṇḍalinī Sādhanā* is also known as *Ṛju Mārga* (straight path). *Lalitā Sahasranāma* mentions three forms of spirituality: *Divyā*, *Mānava* and *Siddhā*.

The different *cakras* (nerve plexuses) have been conceived to be the abodes of different mystical gods and goddesses, who grant different types of mystic power (*Siddhi*) are known as different places of pilgrimage. The top-most *cakra* is known as *Mahāsukha Cakra*. The sole objective of *Tantra Sādhanā* is to cross these different *cakras* and reach the *Mahāsukha Cakra*, the fountainhead of infinite bliss and beatitude.

It is believed that the Bangla literature begins with *Chariyapada*. We have already stated that the *Sahajiya* Cult and the Zen mystic practices are like walking on the razors edge. One of the *Sahajiya* saint has said that it is like, "make the frog dance in the mouth of the snake". In other words the *Sahajiya* saint suggests that great restrain must be practiced by the followers of the cult, who like the snake must resist devouring the frog through when it is dancing in the snake's mouth.

Like Zen Buddhism *Sahajiya* Cult is not an institutionalized religion. Both Zen and *Sahajiya* do not believed in religious denomination. The religious scriptures donot contain the real message of religion. The essence of religion is contained in the inner most being.

धर्मस्य तत्त्वं निहितं गुहायाम्। *Mahābhārata*

Chariyapada is the canonical literature of *Sahajiya* philosophy. It is written like other mystical philosophical text in Twilight language (*Sandhyā Bhāṣā*). *Siddhāchārya's* have composed songs and hyms to express their mustic experience of truth and reality. Chandidas is considered as a great exponent of *Sahajiya* Cult. According to Chandidas Humanity is the highest truth and there is nothing beyond mankind.

Vidyāpati and Roop Goswami are distinguished saints belonging to *Sahajiya* Cult. The central objective of both *Sahajiya* Cult and Zen is to attain self enlightenment. *Chariyapada* and other *Sahajiya* literature have enriched the Bangla, Maithali, Oriya, and Assamese languages.

Nāthaism and Zen

Like Zen Buddhism Nāthaism is based on mysticism. This mystic yogic school was founded by Matsyendranātha, a fisher man from Bengal. Nāthaism is based on Tantrism. Śiva is conceived as supreme God and he occupies supreme position in the Nāthaism. Śiva is the founding father of Tantrism. He is known as *Ādi Guru*. Śiva is deified in Nāthaism. The worship of Śiva is coeval with *Tantras* and Nāthaism. Śiva occupies supreme position in Nāth Cosmogony.

The five mystic saints of Nāthaism are Matsyendranātha, Meenanātha, Gorakhanātha, Kanupā and Churanginātha (*Hadipā*). The whole Nāthaism literatures are the narratives of the *siddhis*. Gorakhanātha is considered as the greatest *Nātha Yogi*. The esoteric school of Nāthaism is based on asceticism, renunciation and *Kuṇḍalinī yoga*. *Mantra*, *Yantra*, and *Kuṇḍalinī* are the cardinal principles of tantric mysticism. *Kuṇḍalinī* is the greatest discovery of *tantra*. It is an esoteric concept. Without awakening of *Kuṇḍalinī* one cannot attend enlightenment.

For the awakening of *Kuṇḍalinī*, incantation of *mantra* (mystic syllable) and practice *yantra* (mystic diagram) are essential. *Mantra* and *Yantra* are the warp and woof of *Yoga Sādhanā*.

Nāthaism and Zen are spirituality. They are not a religion. They do not belong to any religious tradition. *Nātha Yogis* are also called *Kanpathā Yogī*. *Nāthā Yogī* follows strict yogic rules and disciplines. Every *Nāthayogi* would have to take free strict vows (i) To lead a celibate life. (ii) Will not accept any employment and sustain his life by begging. (iii) Observe non-violence.

The evolution of spirituality in India is based on mysticism. The urge for the beyond is the sheet anchor of the Philosophical Culture in India. All the schools of mysticism are unanimous that ultimate reality is beyond the reach of senses and mind. Original source of mysticism is *Tantra*. *Tantric* tradition has exercised great impact on the life and culture of India.

Tantra is a science of religion and philosophy of science. Like Zen Buddhism Nāthaism does not believe in lifeless rituals and religious dogmas. Truth cannot be attained through the exercise of reason. The awakening of the *Kuṇḍalinī* is a great event in the life of *Nāthayogī*. The esoteric process of awakening the *Kuṇḍalinī* has been laid down in Nāthaism. A.K. Bannerjee while explaining the philosophy and esoteric practices of *Nāthaism* writes : "This is often described as the sacred *yātrā* (journey) of awakened *Kuṇḍalinī-Śakti* for the most blissful union with her eternal Beloved Śiva, in the highest region of spiritual experience, *Sahasrāra Chakra*. In the course of this gradual ascent of the psycho-vital energy along the path of *Suṣumnā*, *Yogīs* meet with a number of subtle *cakras*, at particular stages and particular centres, in which they are required to perform particular forms of meditation for particular yogic achievement and which they have to pierce through in order to reach the highest plane of transcendental spiritual experience".[24]

According to the Nāthaism reality is opened to experience of enlightenment which is a state of infinite bliss and beatitude. The *Yogī* experiences the divine effulgence. The *Nāthayogī* and Zen Monk do not indulge in philosophical polemics.

Sufism and Zen

Like Zen, Sufism also belongs to the mystic tradition. The word Sufi is generator to describe the individual practices to attain direct communion between God and man. The all mystic traditions believe in the non-dualism (*advaita*). The word "Sufism" is derived from Arabic word "Suf" which means wool. It refers to the garment which the early Sufi saints used to worn. Sufism does not believe in institutionalize religion. Sufism does not belong to semitic religious tradition. Like Zen Buddhism the aim of Sufism is to attain enlightenment. Enlightenment is a natural state of non-dualism where all distinctions and differences are obliterated in mutual interpenetration between God and man. It is an esoteric dimension of Islam. Some scholars believe that Sufism has Non-Islamic origin.

Rumi and Al-Ghazali are the greatest mystic saints of Sufism. Sufism is a mystic discipline for the interiorazation and intensification of divinity. Classical Sufism is based on asceticism and esotericism. It is a reaction against the attachment to the worldliness of the Caliphate. In the Arabic word "Sufism" is called *Tasawwuf.* This is the mystic aspects of Islam. This is a mystic discipline devoted to understand the reality as natural state of one's own being and existence. There is no difference between the God and the man. This state of mystic unification between God and the man is called enlightenment.

The enlightenment means the attainment of divine effulgence in which all the existing differences are eradicated in the harmonious unification of God and man. In this state of enlightenment the internal conflicts and confusions are obliterated. This is the mystic pilgrimage of man to God. There is a great similarity between the Zen Buddhism and Sufism. Both these sects are based on ontological mysticism. Neither Zen nor Sufism believes in lifeless rituals, dogmas and intellectualization. Zen and the Sufism is pathless path.

Sufi saints are called *Whirling Dervishes*. Sufi saints go on dancing on a circular movement until they attain enlightenment. This is called God — realization. Like Zen, Sufi saints also practice meditation to attain self-realization.

Baul and the Zen

Like Zen Buddhism, Baul is mysticism. Both Zen and the Baul are not institutionalised religion. Both the mystic sects do not believe in religious denomination. According to some Indologists it is an integral part of *Sahajiya* cult. The 'Baul' word is derived from *Sanskrit vatula*, which means enlightened person. It is very difficult to fix the date of its origin. However, the word Baul has been profusely used in *Chaitanya Bhagavat*. According to some scholars it is integral part of *Yoga* and *Chariyapada*.

There are two schools of Baul. According to one school Baul does not live family life. Bauls are fully dependent on alms. They are roaming ascetics. The other school allows to live a family life but they are not attached to worldliness life. Bauls are known as God intoxicated ascetics. The Baul songs speak of long heritage of mysticism of Tantricism and Vaiṣṇavism. It belongs to oral tradition. The lyrics of Baul are based on Non-dualism (*Advaita*). The central objective of Baul is a longing for oneness with God. It speaks of the divinity in man. In the words of Rabindranath Tagore it is "Divinity of Man and Humanity of God". The integral part of the Baul philosophy is that human body is temple of God. Like *Vedānta*, Baul and the Zen also believe that we can attain enlightenment by the purification of human body. *Vedānta* have also given importance to human body and this is why another name of *Brahma Sūtra* is *Śāriraka Sūtra*. The Bauls are very famous for their mystical songs. They use different kind of musical instruments but the most famous is *Ek Tārā* (One string plucked drum). Like Zen, the Baul also believes that a man is hibernated God. God is hidden in the innermost being. We cannot reach or experience the divinity with the help of priest or prophet. The Baul denounces all kinds of religious denominations and fanaticism. The temple and mosque are the greatest detrimental to the path of divine journey. One will have to start his inner divine journey to experience the divine effulgence and enlightenment. Lalan Shah Fakir who is considered as the greatest Baul ascetic has denounced the pilgrimage. He has stated in one of his song whether you go to Kashi or Macca you will return back disappointed and disgraced. By going to Macca you will experience the push of the crowd and if you go to Kashi you would have the same experience and you would spent your life in fruitless journey and would forget your *summum bonum* of life.[25]

Avadhūta Gītā which is considered as the canonical literature of *Vedānta* also denounces the pilgrimage for the seeker of truth. *Avadhūta Gītā* says, "By my making pilgrimage to Thee Thy all — pervasiveness has been destroyed by me. With my meditation Thy transcendence of the mind has been destroyed by me. Thy transcendence of speech has been destroyed by me by my singing Thy praise. Ever forgive me these three sins".[26]

Lalan Shah Fakir says, "those who have known self he alone attains divine wisdom".[27]

The Bauls have exercised significant impact on the culture of the

Bengal. The songs of Lalan Shah Fakir have become the great inspirations for the seekers of truth and God. His songs are based on Ontological Mysticsm and Tantrism. The Zen and the Baul have enriched the mystical culture of human history. The mysticsm of Zen and Baul form the basis of metaphysics of Non-dualism (*Advaita*). The 8th century Persian minstrels are also known as Ba'l. The Bauls songs are the philosophical and cultural manifestation of Tantrism, Sufism, and Buddhism. According to all the mystic tradition reality is one indivisible all comprehensive Absolute. Concept of virtue and vise, bondage and freedom "I" and "mine" does not exist.

Conclusion

Since Indus Valley Civilization (E. 2500 B.C.) founded by Śiva blossom the non-dual (*advaita*) metaphysical and mystical tradition blossomed in 6th century B.C. by the Buddha the Lao Tse Pythagoras and Permendes, is alive in Zen Buddhism, Sufism, *Sahajiya* Cult, Nāthaism, Baul and Pythagoreanism. It speaks of humanities deep confidence and commitment to the ontological mysticism. We are not leaving in natural life. Natural Life is a divine effulgence and salvation. Philosophy is mysticism and mysticism is philosophy. The task of philosophy is to take out the mankind from the darkness of Plato's cave to the light of truth, reality and divine effulgence. This is salivation. Mysticism forms the basis of all civilization and culture. It covers the whole gamut of human existence. Mysticism originated with man. *Advaita* (non-dualism) is a state of spiritual sublimity in which all kinds of existing differences are obliterated not by transcendence and sublation, but by mutual harmonious unification.

Everybody is a enlightened being. To experience the enlightenment one needs only to discard the dualism of mind and body. All of us are endowed with *Buddha*-nature. Awakening is a natural state of our being. We are not living in harmony with our own nature. This is called bondage. This is why we are not experiencing the bliss and the beatitude of *Satori*.

Religion does not contain in scriptures. Essence of religion is contained in inner most being

Phythagoras, Rumi, Kabir, Lalan Shah Fakir, Tilopa, Gorakhanātha and *Bodhidharma* are mystic seers. They have regenerated mankind by their propagation of spiritual humanism and non-dual metaphysical and mystical philosophy of inclusive oneness. They believed in the religion of man devoid of all kind of denominations. They are men of renaissance and real makers of history of human civilization.

Einstein did believe in the existence of God. His conception of God is quite different from the Semetic religion. According to him God is an eternal law that governs the cosmos. Werner Heisenberg agrees with Einstein conception of God as a principle. He writes,

> "Einstein's conception is closer to mine. His God is somehow involved in the immutable laws of nature. Einstein has a feeling for the central order of things. He can detect it in the simplicity of natural laws. We may take it that he felts this simplicity very strongly and directly during his discovery of the theory of relativity. Admittedly, this is a far cry from the comments of religion. I do not believe Einstein is tied to any religious tradition; and I rather think the idea of a personal God is entirely foreign to him. But as far he is concerned there is no split between science and religion : the central order is part of the subjective as well as the objective realm, and this strikes me as being a far better starting point".

Maxplanck the founding father of quantum mechanics is of the opinion that there is no contradiction between religion and science. He believes that both are perfectly compatible. Religion consists of two parts, i.e. (i) Spirituality and (ii) Mythology. Spirituality is the core of religion. Planck, Heisenberg, Einstein and Schrödinger have used the word religion, in the sense of divinity and value not as ritualism and mythology. Heisenberg writes about his discussions in the evening that was held during the Solvay Conference with the other scientist such as Wolfgang, Pauli and Pauldirac about religion and God. "From some of Planck's utterances it would seem that he sees no contradiction between religion and science, indeed that he believes the two is perfectly compatible". If we examine the statements and discoveries of scientist and the vision of the mystic seers we come to the conclusion that reality is mystical and metaphysical. Scientists have expressed the ultimate truth and reality in different linguistic form but refer to the same truth. Science and spirituality are one in ultimate analysis and examinations as the basis of both is ontological mysticism.

According to spiritual humanism Brahman of Hinduism, Allah of Sufism, Tao of Taoism and *Śūnyatā* of Buddhism are the ultimate reality. Reality is cosmic consciousness. It is the goal source, substance and substratum of whole universe. The cosmic consciousness is Cosmos. It is called Buddha nature in Buddhism. Divine melody of mystical songs liberates the singers from the dark night of soul. Asceticism is an integral part of Zen Buddhism. Zen Buddhism, Pythagoreanism, Sufism, Nāthaism, *Sahajiya* Cult and Bauls mystical hyms and songs are used to cleanse the soul from all kinds of mental ratiocination and false subjectivity. The body is the temple of divinity. Meditation is discipline employed to purify all the cells of the body so that it could bear the dawn of divine effulgence which is thousand times more brilliant than the Sun. It is the light of the enlightenment. It is the state of infinite bliss.

Salvation is *Summum Bonnum* of human life in the all schools of mysticism. The core concept of mysticism is non-dualism. The non-dualism (*advaita*) is the basis of Pythagoreanism, Sufism, Nāthaism, *Sahajiya* Cult, Baul Sect and Zen Buddhism. Zen Buddhism is Profound metaphysical and Mystical Sect. Zen is not a religion. It is spirituality. It is an intuitional Science. It is a pathless path.

Notes

1. *Nature and the Greeks, Science and Humanism*, Erwin Schrödinger, Cambridge University Press, 1954, 1952, p. 108.
2. *Zen Masters of China, The First Step East*, Richard Bryan McDaniel, Tuttle Publishing, 2012, p. 38.
3. *The Essentials of Tao,* Tao Te Ching, Translated and presented by Thomas Cleary, Herper San Francisco, 1993, Verse 56.
4. Okakuro-Kakuzo, *The Book of Tea* (published by Fox Duffield, New York).
5. Erwin Schrödinger, *op. cit.*, p.125.
6. *On Indian Mahayana Buddhism*, D. T. Suzuki, p. 122.
7. *The Tao of Physics*, Fritjof Capra, p. 89.
8. *The Central Philosophy of Buddhism*, T.R.V. Murti, pp. 142-143.
9. *Yoga Immortality and Freedom*, Mircea Eliade, Bollingen Series, Princeton, 1958, p. xx.
10. *Śiva Sūtras*, The Yoga of Supreme Identity, Jaideva Singh, Motilal Banarasidass Publishers, Delhi, p. xxxvii.
11. The Path of Purification (*Visuddhimagga*), by Bhadantacariya Buddhaghosa, Translated from the Pāli by Bhikkhu Nanamoli. Buddhist Publication Society, Kandy Sri Lanka, 1975, p. 587.

12. *Lao Tzu and Taoism*, Max Kaltenmark, Translated by the French; by Roger Greaves, Stanford University Press, Stanford, California, 1969, p. 52.
13. Tao Te Ching, *op. cit.*, p. 18.
14. *Zen and Japanese Culture*, Daisetz T. Suzuki, Princeton University Press, Princeton and Oxford, p. 6.
15. *Tattvakaumudi*, (ed.) Ganganatha Jha, p. 1.
16. *Bhāmati*, (ed.) Bala Sastri, pp. 1-2.
17. *Zen Masters of China, The First Step East, Zen Stories Collected and Retold,* Richard Bryan McDaniel, Tuttle Publishing, Tokyo, 2012, p. 67.
18. *The New Encyclopaedia Britannica*, Vol. 3, by Encyclopedia Britannica Inc. 1976, U.S.A., p. 386.
19. *Encyclopaedia of Buddhism*, Vol. III, by G.P. Malalasekera, 1972, Published by the Government of Sri Lanka, Government Press, Ceylon, p. 194.
20. *Tractatus Logico-Philosophicus,* Wittgenstein, Routledge Classics, 2001, p. 89.
21. Andrew Juniper, *Wabi Sabi the Japanese Art of Impermanence*, p. 159, Tuttle Publishing, Tokyo, 2003.
22. *From Physics and Beyond*, by Werner Heisenberg (Harper & Row, 1971)
23. *Early Greek, Philosophy,* p. 108.
24. *Philosophy of Gorakhnath*, p. 172. Mahant Digvijay Nath Trust, Gorakhnath Temple, Gorakhpur.
25. *The Songs of Lalan Shah Fakir*, (Hindi), p. 201, Muchkund Dubey, Sahitya Academic Publication, New Delhi, 2017.

    मक्का जाकर धक्का खाकर,
    जाना चाहो अब काशी धाम।
    इसी फेर में दिन कट गया,
    तय न कर पाए सही स्थान।

26. *Avadhūta Gītā*, Chapt. VIII, verse 1, p. 162, Sri Ramakrishna Math, Chennai, 2015.

    त्वद्यात्रया व्यापकता हता ते
    ध्यानेन चेतःपरता हता ते।
    स्तुत्या मया वाक्परता हता ते
    क्षमस्व नित्यं त्रिविधापराधान् ।। 1।।

27. *Songs of Lalan Shah Fakir*, p. 78.

    आत्मतत्व जिसने जाना,
    दिव्य ज्ञानी वही हुआ।
    कुवृक्ष से सुंदर फल पाया,
    मेरे मन का मोह मिटा ना।

CHAPTER 2
Introduction

Buddhist Background of Zen Buddhism

Zen Buddhism derives its name from the Sanskrit word *Dhyāna* (meditation). The word *Dhyāna* is known in Chinese *Ch'an* and Japanese Zen. This school of Buddhism emphasises meditation as the way to experience the immediate awareness of ultimate reality. Zen is the experience of ultimate reality, realization of which is called *Satori*. However, the ultimate reality is beyond the reach of mind and senses. Hinduism also describes ultimate reality as *"Neti-Neti"* not this, not this. Zen Buddhism believes that the positive description of the intrinsic nature of reality is not possible. It cannot be grasped through senses and understanding, like Upaniṣadic teachings.[1] Like Upaniṣadic mysticism the experience of the ultimate reality is direct, total and integral. This immediate awareness or the enlightenment is known as *Bhāvanāmaya Paññā* in *Theravāda* Buddhism. This state of spiritual sublimity is what is called suchness or isness in *Mahāyāna* tradition. In Japanese it is known as "*kono-mama*" or "*Sono-mama*." In Chinese it is called "*Chih-mo*" or "*Shik-mo*", or in Sanskrit the same reality is known as "Tathatā." The mystic experience of the ultimate reality takes a man to the state of *isness*, where he thoroughly purged from all sorts of intellectual and moral consideration. This state of spiritual sublimity is to be experienced and not to be explained through a language.

The Zen Buddhism was developed from the teachings of *Laṅkāvatāra sūtra* according to which all beings possess the Buddha-nature. This Buddha-nature is often equated with "*Śūnya*" (emptiness) the realization of which is enlightenment. The realization of the ultimate truth or reality takes men beyond the dualism of subject and object.

Bodhidharma who visited China in A.D. 520 is known as the first patriarch of Ch'an school in China. However, according to Indian *Mahāyāna* Buddhist tradition there is a line of 28 Patriarches from Lord Buddha to *Bodhidharma*, the founder of Zen school. They are as follows:

1. Śākyamuni, 2. Mahākassapa, 3. Ānanda, 4. Savaṁsa, 5. Upāgupta, 6. Dhṛtaka, 7. Miśchaka, 8. Buddhānandī, 9. Bodhamitra, 10. Bhikkhu Pārśva, 11. Puṇyayashas, 12. Aśvaghōṣa, 13. Bhikkhu Kapimala, 14. Nāgārjuna, 15. Kanadeva, 16. Ārya Rāhulata, 17. Saṅghānandī, 18. Saṅghayashas, 19. Kumārata, 20. Jayata, 21. Vasubandhu, 22. Manura, 23. Haklenayasas, 24. Bhikkhu Siṁha, 25. Vasasita, 26. Puṇyamitra, 27. Prajñātāra, and 28. Bodhidharma.

According to this tradition, once Śākyamuni was addressing the congregation of his disciples at the mount of *Grijakuṭī* at Rājgir. He simply lifted a banquet of flowers which was presented to him by one of his lay disciple no body understood the spiritual and the mystic implication of this, except the Venerable Mahākassapa who quietly smiled at the master. Venerable Mahākassapa could comprehend the language of the Silence of the Master. After this Lord Buddha made a spiritual declaration, that he has handed over to venerable Mahākassapa the most secret treasure of inner spirituality and transcendental teachings which is known as "Zen Buddhism."[2] From the philosophical point of view it is of no spiritual importance whether this historical event has really taken place or not. However, it is on historical record the venerable Mahākassapa succeeded Lord Buddha as the head of the Buddhist faith. A detailed history of Zen Buddhist succession has been enumerated in a book entitled "*Transmission of the Lamp*", written by Li-Tsum-Hsui in 1029.

According to some scholars, the Zen Buddhism as a distinct School of *Mahāyāna* tradition was born with *Bodhidharma's* visit to China in A.D. 520, and he was acclaimed as the first patriarch. After *Bodhidharma* his Chinese disciple Hui-ko (468-593 A.D.), became the Second patriarch of Zen School. He was succeeded by Seng-Ts'an who died in A.D. 606. There is no detailed historical account of his life, however, this third patriarch left a remarkable collection of Zen sayings in poetic form known as "*Hsing-hsimming.*" The poems of this Zen-master are pregnant with mystical and philosophical ideas like Kabir. Tao-hsin (580-651) succeeded *Shing-hsimming* and is known as the fourth patriarch. However, the historic visit of

Bodhidharma to China brought a spiritual renaissance, and Buddhism became the living religion of China. Buddhism assimilated in itself some of the finer concept of Confucianism and Taoism which made this new Buddhism richer and fuller. This new Buddhism which put more emphasis on meditation is known as Zen Buddhism. However, the role of the Zen Patriarchies in shaping this new Buddhism and making it a living religious force is a fact of history. Some of the patriarchies were men of great spiritual attainments.

Houng-Jen (601-675) the fifth patriarch is considered as the spiritual father of Hui-Neng the sixth patriarch, whose spiritual attainment is equated with Bodhidharma. Hui-Neng is called second Bodhidharma. It is the spiritual leadership of this great Zen-master (sixth patriarch) which provided the philosophical and mystical background for blossoming this new Buddhism during the T'ang Dynasty of China into an independent school of Buddhism. The sermon and the teachings of Hui-Neng are simply profound and pregnant with deep philosophical ideas. Teachings of Zen-masters became the fountain of new philosophical ideas and moral regeneration.

Hui-Neng died at the age of 76 in the year A.D. 712, when he received the robe of Bodhidharma from the hands of his master Houng-Jen. Houng-Jen observed that Hui-Neng was greater than the life-size Zen-master. It was for this reason that, there was no acknowledged seventh patriarch.

According to one tradition there were only five patriarches and after the death of Houng-Jen the fifth patriarch, the schism occurred between the believers of the Northern School founded by Shen-Shui and the Southern School of Hui-Neng.[3] According to other tradition Hui-Neng was the sixth patriarch and he was acclaimed as one of the greatest Zen-master that world has produced. According to this tradition after the death of Hui-Neng, the Zen Buddhism was splitted into several schools many of which still exist in China and Japan.[4] According to this tradition one of the branch of Zen Buddhism is known as Sōtō School and another branch which claimed it descends from the teaching of Houiai-Jang, the successor of Hui-Neng is known as Rinzai School. The prominent successors of Hui-Neng were the acknowledged Zen-masters Hsi-yun of Huang Po and Hui-Hai.

From the available historical account of the Chism it seems the concept of enlightenment and its method as well as way for its attainment became the point of philosophical dispute and difference, which resulted into the split of Zen Buddhism into different schools. According to one school enlightenment must be attained gradually. This school is known as Northern school founded by Shen-hsui. On the other hand Southern school believes that the true wisdom is undifferentiated and it can be attained spontaneously. This school does not give any importance to rituals and scriptures. This school believes the secret of the knowledge passed from master to pupil like Hindu-traditions and adopts iconoclastic attitude to the Buddha. The two schools have fundamentally different views of the Buddha-nature. Southern School believes that, if all the things contain the *Buddha*-nature the Buddha could be equated with the heap of dung. In the struggle of superiority the Southern school won out and its superiority was pronounced in authentic Chinese *Ch'an* texts, and its founder Hui-Neng was proclaimed as the sixth patriarch. From all accounts Hui-Neng was a great Zen-master. In course of time, two prominent branches of Zen Buddhism were developed, which was known as Rinzai School in Japan (Len-Chi-in Chinese) and the Sōtō School in Japan (Ts'ao-Lung, in China).

The Southern school particularly Rinzai School developed a technique for conquering the mind from the dualism of subject and object to attain *Nirvāṇa* (enlightenment) by throwing the mind of its familiar track of logical reasoning to make it ready for meditative insight. This method is known as *Koan*. This technique is employed through paradoxical question and answer for the purpose of inducing the practitioner and to realize that all conceptualizations are wrong and insipid. This realization suddenly lifts a man from the mundane existence and it paves the path for the dawn of enlightenment. The *Koans* are accompanied by shouts and stapes from the Zen-masters to provoke anxiety and anguish which results into sudden realization of the nature of suchness. The Zen-master imparts instructions of meditation to rid the mind from all notions. This Zen school incorporated in itself the Christian doctrine of "work is worship." In Zen Buddhism this doctrine is known as *Hui-Hai* which means "the monk who does not work will not eat." The introduction of *Hui-Hai* doctrine transformed the Zen school from the parasitic Buddhist living to economic self-sufficiency.

According to some historians the Zen Buddhism is influenced by Taoism. David L. Sills observed that "Taoism with its naturalistic mysticism, provided an important outlet of the socially induced tensions and the pressures of conventional civilization."[5] According to him it was equally significant that the *hsuin-hsueh* (mysterious learning) esoteric gnosis with a comparatively sophisticated metaphysics. The concept of Buddha-nature and Tao represents the same reality. The *Taoist* has also incorporated the *Koan* technique in an endeavour to find out the truth. On the other hand the Zen Buddhism is greatly influenced by the *Taoist* emphasis on natural life. However, the Indian Buddhism is the main source of inspiration for the emergence of Zen School. The technique of meditation and the concept of Buddha-nature have definitely been borrowed from the original Indian Buddhism, which suited the Chinese and the Japanese mental framework.

The Zen came to Japan in seventh century, the work of the two Zen-masters Eisai and Dōgen, made it a living religious force. The work of Eisai is so original and profound that a separate school of Zen Buddhism was founded after his thought which is known as Rinzai School. Eisai was so much inspired by Buddhism that he visited China to restore the originality and pure form of Buddhistic teachings. After his returned, he introduced strict meditational system based on the use of the *koan*-phrases. Eisai also introduced Socio-religious elements in this new Buddhism. H◦ taught that, it was the moral and the social responsibility of the Zen ιɔ defend the state. The observance of the ceremonical rules and rituals and the offer of prayers and incantations were introduced into this new system, which attracted the *Samurai* class (warrior class) of Japan, the influence of which could be traced in the arts of Archery and Swordsmanship. The Zen Buddhism became very popular amongst the upper classes in the beginning.[6] In the beginning it gained ground among the aristocratic families of Japan. Zen Buddhism covered latter on the whole gamut of Japanese life. Its impacts can be traced in the "No–play" in Japanese poetry, *Ikebana*, flower arrangement, *cho-no-ya* tea ceremonies all of which would emphasise on grace and spontaneity.

Dōgen, the founder of *Sōtō* school in the thirteenth century also joined the *Tendai* monastery of mount *Hiei* in search of the truth and the meaning of life. Like *Eisai*, he also went to China, and took lessons from Zen-master. After his returned to Japan, he introduced *Zazen* sitting straight as a mystic technique for the attainment of enlightenment. Unlike his teacher he studied scriptures and analysed the philosophical meanings of the religious texts, and he did not hesitate in criticising the religious scriptures which were not in tune with this new faith.

The central objectives of the Zen-masters were to restore Buddhism in health and purity. From its very inception the aim of this new sect was the attainment of "*Satori*." From the very beginning the founding fathers were not interested in writing about the technique of meditation descriptions of the progressive stages and doctrinal implication of the experience of the suchness. It is a debatable point whether the meditational technique was taken from Indian teachers or it has been borrowed from Taoist practice of meditation which were prevalent in China in the earlier days. Dr. Hu Shin says: that classical way of Zen meditation in setting posture is of Indian Buddhist origin and the walking meditation has been developed by Chinese Zen-masters.[7] It is believed that through walking meditation, the practitioner wanted to attain realization through contact with nature on long walking trips from one mountain temple to another. It was a general practice among the young Zen monks to undertake the long pilgrimages in search for suitable *Guru* (teacher) with whom they could establish *INNEN* the (true rapport) and the older monks also used to set out on pilgrimages after the attainment of enlightenment in order to verify their own wisdom and understanding with some established Grand Zen-masters.

In the seventh and eighth centuries the Zen enlightened masters used to settle in a remote mountain side in a little hut often made by his own hands. Like Indian saints from the historical account of the early Zen Buddhism practice in China it is evident that the line of transmission of meditation was carried from Indian traditions; like Indian traditions, the young seeker after truth used to construct their own huts near the huts of the enlightened Zen-masters and kept themselves engaged in meditation receiving instructions and serving their masters. With the increase of the Zen practitioners the permanent building were constructed and a new culture of temple building were introduced to house the Zen practitioners. The meditation and the physical labours were the chief forms of activities. The code of conduct were developed to discipline the life of the practitioners. These fixed rules and regulations were enforced like the code of conduct of the *Āśrama* life of the Indian *Gurus*.

In these hermits the Zen-masters use to give talks at regular intervals which is known in Japanese "*Jōdo*" which means ascending the hall. The masters used to occupy a raised seat in the temple's halls or the court-yard and discuss the salient features of Buddhism more or less in an informal manner employing mostly the dilect of the local people. In these sittings the questions and the answers sessions were held to clarify and elucidate the paradoxical lessons of Zen meditation. These questions and answers session is known as "*mondō*."

Zen Buddhism is one of the living sects of *Mahāyāna* tradition. The *Mahāyāna* Buddhism has incorporated in its philosophical and religious system some of the moral and the religious customs and teachings of the land where it became the faith of the people. And it is no wonder that the present form of Zen Buddhism has imbibed the moral teachings of Confucianism the meditational practice of Taoism and the religious roots and the rituals of *Shintoism*. Present Zen Buddhism has formed a single interlocking system for the specialized satisfaction of a wide range of personal and social needs. The some family that takes an infant to a *Shinto* Shrine for a Baptismal ceremony without any sense of conflict, have funeral rites conducted by Buddhist monks and maintain family ancestral worship and ethical standards largely dominated by Confucian values.[8] The Confucianism, Taoism and Buddhism offered systematic critique of the old values and redefined the meaning of existence and life. The synthesis of these three major schools of thoughts resulted in the resurrection of man and the emergence of new social order within framework of universal and transcendental thoughts. This ushers in a new cultural reconstruction and renaissance which attracted the imaginative and the progressive mind of Chinese and Japanese people. The rational political system of Confucianism with its cosmological metaphysics reinforced the worldly institutions and obligations and goals of individual and the society. In this process of cultural metamorphosis, a new philosophical and religious system was born. A new sotoriology placing infinite worth and value on the legitimacy of personal salvation, in the present world of anguish, alienation was introduced. David L. Sells says, that "the most remarkable synthesis of Chinese and Indians values was achieved in the meditation school of Ch'an (Zen). While it was based on the auto-soteriological principles of Yōgic action, its leadership developed a unique meditative technique, which stressed practical, non-discursive, and naturalistic media for attaining enlightenment."[9]

The emergence of Zen Buddhism evokes liberating thoughts to the mutilated reality of insipid philosophy and religion divorced from social reality. The function of Philosophy according to Zen Buddhism is to promote the art of life. The speculations about the good-life, the just-society, peace and prosperity obtain increasingly realistic content on the new religious and ethical grounds created by Zen Buddhism. The truth of the religious propositions is to be determined by their socio-political content and their experimental value. The origin of Zen in Śākyamuni's attaining *Nirvāṇa* (enlightenment) and the continuous efforts to transmit this truth to the following generation have been given little consideration by the modern man under the impact of modern scientific knowledge and technological advancement. The revival of meditational practice and the old ethical values by Zen-masters and their re-definition is welcome step to coordinate mental operation with social reality.

Notes

1. *Yato vaco nivartante aprāpya manasā saha. – Taittirīya Upaniṣad*, II.4.1.
2. *Essays in Zen Buddhism*, Vol. I, p. 165; T.D. Suzuki, *Living Zen*, Robert Linssen, George Allen & Unwin Ltd., 1954, p.40.
3. *Encyclopaedia Britannica*, p. 386.
4. *Living Zen, op. cit.*
5. *International Encyclopaedia of the Social Sciences*, Vol. I, David L. Sills. New York: The MacMillan Company & The Free Press, Reprint Edition, 1972, p. 176.
6. *Encyclopaedia of Religion and Ethics* (James Hastings), Vol. IV, New York: Charles Scribner's Jons Morrison and U.S.A. & Canada: Gibb Limited, p. 704.
7. *Zen a Method for Religious Awakening* (Ruth Fuller Sasaki) Kyoto, Japan: Nissha Printing Co. Ltd., 1969, p. 8.
8. *International Encyclopaedia of the Social Sciences*, Vol. I, p. 165.
9. *Ibid.*, Vol. I, p. 178.

Teaching of the Buddha (B.C. 563-483)
Ancient Schools

- 1 Sthāviravāda
  - Theravāda (Continues in Ceylon and Southeast Asia)
  - Sarvās thivāda Pri-t'an Chu-she (China) Kusha (Japan)
- 2 Sautrāntika
- 3 Mahisāsaka
  Dharmaguptaka
- 4 Vinaya Schools :
  Lu (China)
  Ritsu (Japan)
- 5 Transitional schools :
  Mahāsaṅghika
  Lokōttaravāda
  Vatsiputriya,
  Sammatiya
  Satyasiddhi
  - Mahāyāna
  - Ch'eng-Shin (China) Jojitsu (Japan)

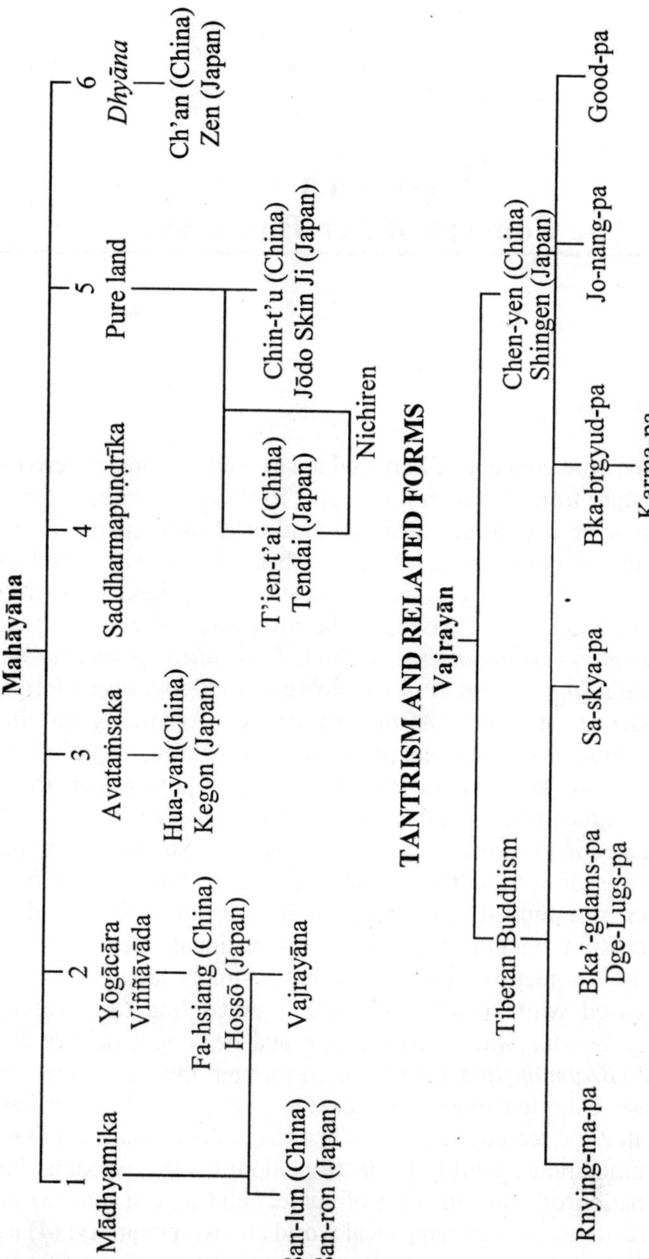

Source: The New Encyclopaedia Britannica Macropaedia, Vol. 3, 15th Edition, 1975, U.S.A., p. 377.

CHAPTER 3
The Concept of Zen Buddhism

Zen and *Dhyāna*

Dhyāna is the core concept of Zen Buddhism. Zen Buddhism derives its nomenclature from this central concept. To attain *Nirvāṇa* does not mean to know or understand *Buddha*-mind or *Buddha*-nature in an intellectual or objective sense. It means to become one with it and to reveal *Tathatā* in its totality to attain this state of spiritual sublimity. The concept of *Dhyāna* is based on the *Mahāyāna Sūtras*; such as *Prajñāpāramitā*, *Vajrasamādhī* and *Vimala Kīrtinirdesa*. *Bodhidharma*'s *Dhyāna* theory of two entrances and four deeds forms the quintessence of above *Mahāyāna Sūtras*. According to the Chinese tradition *Bodhidharma* practiced "wall-gazing" meditation for nine long years and attained tremendous occult power apart from attaining enlightenment. During this period *Bodhidharma* kept himself engaged in deep meditation at the *Shao-Lin-Ssu* temple on the mount Saung-shan and during these periods he neither read any scriptures nor worshipped any images simply sat throughout the day with leg crossed facing wall. This meditational technique of *Bodhidharma* is sometimes misunderstood as simply facing the wall with leg-crossed while practicing *Dhyāna*. According to Carolnie Rhys Davids Buddha was a fervent *jhan* and he sought neither the cosmic soul (*Brahman*) nor God (*Īśvara*) through the *Jhāna* that he practiced, nor exhorted others to seek them. *Poṭṭhapāda-Sutta* has formulated that the technique of Buddhist meditation aimed at (1) to purify the mind and sensibility from temptation; (2) to overcome the dualistic function of mind in form of subject and object; and (3) to remove all relations with the empirical world and with memory; (4) to attain the bliss of pure consciousness. Through the practice of these four stages of *Dhyāna* one reaches the summit of consciousness, which is followed by the practice of *Samāpatti*. According to Mircea Eliade Buddhist "meditation" was a means of "mystical" experimentation, a way of access to suprasensible realities, and not an uniomystica. This yogic experience prepared the monk for a "super knowledge" (*abhijña*) whose final goal was "*Nirvāṇa*."[1]

Thus, we find the meditation has always been considered as the way to immediate awareness of ultimate reality or suchness by all the schools of *Mahāyāna Buddhism*. The over emphasis on meditation as special technique and doctrines with Taoist influence has emerged as Zen Sect, generally considered a specifically Chinese product.[2]

However, the psychological and the metaphysical basis of *Dhyāna* is contained in the *Laṅkāvatāra Sūtra,* according to which all things are rooted in the mind or dialectical function of thought and mind is the result of erroneous thinking of dualistic existence of subject and object. To overcome this dualistic function and to remove erroneous thinking and identification of mind with physical and mental objects which is the root cause of bondage and attachment is the object of meditation. The *Dhyāna* is a technique through which the practitioner cuts asunder the trammels of *Māyā* (ignorance) and paves path for immediate awareness of reality. The theory of two-entrances and four deeds of *Bodhidharma* is a technique of *Dhyāna* which is called in *Mahāyāna* mind-tranquilization and consists of four suchnesses. The *Encyclopaedia of Buddhism* says, "The first of the two Entrances, Entrance by Reasons means (1) to receive the law from a Master and believe that all living things have the same True (Buddha), Nature; (2) to meditate on this idea and by having an unshakable faith in it, became one with it, so that the distinction between oneself and others as well as between the unenlightened man and the Buddha are eliminated; and (3) not to rely completely on the printed word, but to come naturally to truth and dwell peacefully and contentedly in it."[3] We think the entrance by reason does not mean just to receive the law from the master and believe that all living things have the same *Buddha*-nature as has been enumerated by some scholars, because *Bodhidharma*'s whole doctrines of wall gazing is based on the theory that one should not become the slave of scriptural teaching, but to experience the truth which is beyond the reach of senses and mind. The wall is metaphorically used, which means exclusion from defilements and erroneous thoughts. Wall gazing personifies the attainment of a state of mental tranquillity and spiritual sublimity.

The entrance by Reason consists of four "deeds": (1) the deed of retribution; (2) the deed of Dependent upon Causation; (3) the deed of non-seeking; and (4) the deed of following the *Dharma*. The first deed emphasise the universal existence of suffering. It teaches that when one experiences suffering one should realizes that it is because of his past actions. The second deed reminds the teaching of *Vajrasamādhī-sūtra*, that mind should not be at work. Deed of dependence of Causation highlights the Buddhist cardinal doctrines of law of Causation known as *Paṭiccaṁsamppāda*. The fourth and the last deed signifies the *Mahāyāna* concept of *Śūnya*. The deed of following the *Dharma* means, "that all aspects of *Dharma* possesses a pure nature and *Śūnya*. Our practice of the *Dharma* must be based upon the principle that neither sentient beings nor lifeless matter are endowed with a permanent unchanging soul. We should strive simultaneously for the Enlightenment of other as well as ourselves and should be free from actions for personal gain alone. The words in the *Vajrasamādhī-sūtra* "cast aside the idea of a soul, work for the emancipation of all living things, be above (birth and death), go beyond external form, do not discriminate by taking this and rejecting that", probably correspond to this fourth deed.[4]

After the spread of Buddhism in China it was transformed into many schools and sects after coming in contact with Confucianism and Taoism. A lot of Buddhist treatises were produced by the scholars which claimed as original teachings of the Buddha. Most of these treatises and canons were based on the teachings of some of the *Sūtra* of *Tripiṭaka* and claiming that the teachings of these *Sūtras* contain the whole truth of Buddhism which aimed at experiencing Buddha-mind through the practice of *Zazen* and upholding the importance and the sacredness culture of Buddhism by integrating the meditational technique of *Bodhidharma* with down to earth philosophy of China.

The method and technique of *Dhyāna* vary in different schools, but it has been universally accepted as esoteric method of mental culture for the attainment of *Nirvāṇa*. Different forms of meditation have been discovered for the man of different dispositions. According to Mr. M. Anesaki and J. Takahusu there are several methods preparatory meditation according to the ability of meditationers. A quick temper novice should practice the meditation on love (*Pāli: Mettā bhāvanā*), in which he has to regard all sentient beings as his parents or brothers desiring their happiness and welfare, as all the good he seeks for himself. A novice who needs concentration of attention should practice at first the method of counting the numbers inspiration and expiration (*Pāli: Ānāpāna sati* corresponding to the *Prāṇāyāma* of the *Yōgāṅga*).[5] Some kind of practice of meditation is considered essential for Buddhists. The practice of *Kammaṭṭhāna* (analytic meditation) is considered preparatory to the practice of right meditation which was culminated into a sect of Zen Buddhism.

The chief characteristic of the Zen Buddhism is that it does not give any evidence to abstractions and concepts and it lives in facts. Zen is a concrete philosophy and it lives in facts. The object of Zen meditation is to integrate the part with the whole, the conscious with the unconscious mind and in this process of unification *Satori* is experienced. This process of unification has been termed as an act of walking on with no-path no-walker and no-goal. This non-sensical statement contains the super sense and awareness that though the intellect is a brilliant tool to understand the language game of thoughts, but there is something where one has to maintain silence. Wittgenstein has rightly observed that, what we cannot speak about we must consign to silence, but he still believes what we cannot speak about exists.[6] What he means that reality is not to be spoken in language, but it is to be experienced because it is the mystical. We can understand the enigmatic teachings of Zen Buddhism with a metaphor, to cross a river a raft is necessary, but after crossing the river raft is left behind, likewise to unfold the riddle of life thought and reasons are necessary tools. But thought sometimes fails to communicate and comprehend which is the state of thoughtlessness or suchness the intellect serves its purpose by pointing towards the unknown and unknowable. Zen-master would say that if you want to attain *Satori*, you dissociate yourself with concepts and abstractions. Thus, the process of *Dhyāna* is a process of freeing the mind from all kinds of dispositions which is called in Zen terminology emptying oneself. There is a famous saying of the Zen-masters:

> "Those who know do not speak;
> Those who speak do not know."

Zen as a Spiritual Discipline

The Buddha kept mum when he was questioned about the unconditions. Vacchagotta could not understand the Buddha's reasons of maintaining silence. However, the many scholars and thinkers have wrongly construed the Buddha's silence as agnosticism. The Buddha was quite conversant with philosophical speculations and he was aware of the fact that reality cannot be conceived in empirical terms. There was justification both spiritual and logical in rejecting speculative metaphysics. Professor Radhakrishnan says, If the Buddha declined to define the nature of the Absolute or if he contented himself with negative definitions, it is only to indicate that absolute being is above all determinations. "Why, then, did Buddha not admit in express terms the reality of the absolute? Buddha refused to describe the absolute, for that would be to take a step out of the world of reality the legitimacy of which he was the first to contest in others. The absolute is not a matter of empirical observation. The world of experience does not reveal the absolute anywhere within its limits.[7] The Buddha was quite conscious about the insurmountable difficulties (*Ādīnavam-Sampassamāno*) in describing the reality which was indescribable, and this is why he considered *tathatā* (reality) is beyond the dualism of subject end object. The reality can be realized only through non-intellectual mode, called *Prajñāpāramitā.* And thus, Buddhism from its very inception was a way of life and a spiritual discipline to realize enlightenment which was considered as culmination of the spiritual quest of each and every individual. Buddhism was never an institutionalized religion and denominational in character. It was developed as a spiritual discipline to rid man from the bondage of suffering. Buddhism believes that there is no God outside the universe who has created it and created man. According to *Mahāyāna* Buddhism universe and man are one indissoluble existence that is *tathatā.* Everything is a temporary manifestation of *tathatā* in different forms and all activities that take place from birth to death, from love and hate, creation and destruction are nothing, but temporary manifestation of *tathatā* in activity. Each one of us possesses temporary individuality which is neither true nor a false ego created by nuisance (*māyā*—ignorance). According to *Mahāyāna* our temporary individuality is an extension of universal reality which is called *Dharmakāya.* Zen Buddhism believes that this undivided personality cannot be realized by intellect. This realization of the suchness (*tathatā*) can be brought about through the awakening of *Prajñāpāramitā*, which is intrinsic to all men, we cannot apply to empirical experience as we do in science. The speculative metaphysics has rid itself from this limitation as it does not depend on empirical verification. However, it views a reality from a particular view point according to its own system and pattern of thought and tends to become dogmatic. And thus the whole philosophical system suffers from this dogmatism which the Buddha called *diṭṭhivāda*. According to Buddhism the reality is to be experienced here and now. The spiritual discipline for awakening this intellectual intuition (*Prajñāpāramitā*) is meditation. Zen Buddhism has been developed out of the quest for the spiritual discipline for awakening the dormant divinity and intuitive wisdom through meditation which provided a spiritual discipline verified through the century for accomplishing it. The philosophical stand point taken by Zen Buddhism should not be confused as revival of *Theravāda,* but retaining the basic teachings of *Śākyamuni* that *Attadīpo bhāva* (Be a lamp unto yourself). Every man must work out his own authentic existence by attaining the religious experience of awakening for himself. *Śākyamuni* occupies supreme place of veneration in Zen Monastery as he is viewed by this sect as the embodiment of original Buddhist teachings.

Zen Buddhism observes rules of spiritual discipline strictly. Spiritual discipline is the fundamental of the supreme-Bodhi, discipline begets immutability and immutability begets wisdom. There is no possibility to self-cultivation, without practicing spiritual discipline. The *Suraṅgama Sutta* which lists four kinds of purity observes that cultivation of *Samādhi* is not possible without practicing of spiritual discipline in letter and spirit.

From the early days of Zen in China in the seventh and eighth centuries there was a practice that an enlightened Zen-masters would reside in a little hut, often prepared by themselves in a remote mountain side. The seekers would build-up their own huts nearby to receive the teachings from the masters. The student would observe the instructions received by the master. Students would seek an audience with master known as *Sanzen* in which the master would give lesson on *Koan* to meditate. To establish an *innen* (rapport) with master is essential for solving the *Koan* through the particular type of meditation known as *kufu.* It is believed that every *koan* has a classical answer. When the answer of *koan,* is an agreement with the classical answer the student would be deemed to have solved the *koan* according to Zen tradition. The whole system of receiving instructions from the Zen-masters known as *Roshi* on meditation to solve different *koan*s is very personal and based on the strict observance of spiritual discipline and a code of conduct.

The Verbal and Actional Aspect of Zen

Verbal

Zen Buddhism is considered as a religion of self-reliance (Japanese *jiyu* and Chinese *tsu-yu*) and self-being (Japanese *Lizai* and Chinese *Tzu-tsai*). This state of self-reliance and self-being is a state of freedom which is the outcome of *nirvāṇa*. The attainment of *nirvāṇa* is the quintessence of Buddhism. Without *nirvāṇa* there is no Buddhism. Zen Buddhism is considered *nirvāṇa* (Japanese *Satori*) as the *summum bonum* of human life. It enumerates two ways – Verbal and Actional for the realization of *Satori*.

The verbalism of Zen Buddhism has its own history and philosophy. It is completely different from the normal semantics of linguistic philosophy. Language is a method of communication. Human beings cannot live without language game. The language game prevalent in a particular culture depicts the people's forms of life lived and experienced in that particular cultural traditions. However, the concept of language cannot be defined. There are no analogous rules by which we can determine the use of a word or a sentence in a given context. A triangle can be defined as figure having three angles and three state lines. But we cannot defined language in the same vein. In logic we know P and not P is as contradiction, however and, from contradiction we can deduced whatever we like. But in question like "Is he a good painter?" If someone answer both "Yes and no" he would be understood as he ought to have been understood without involving himself in any disastrous contradiction, because, "the law of contradiction does not apply to human beings." The Zen is a spiritual experience. The Zen-masters have resorted to language to communicate others and to themselves. Zen Buddhism has developed its own verbalism to communicate the concrete spiritual experience. It is said that the Zen verbalism violate all the rules of semantics and put oneself in enigmatic situation.

The linguistic problems faced by the modern analytical philosophers and that of the Zen practitioners are similar. The modern philosophical problems arises out of misunderstanding of the logic of the language. Philosophical understanding is required to see the problem caused by the misunderstanding of the language. The aim of philosophical reasoning according to Wittgenstein is complete clarity. Complete clarity means the disappearance of the problem and not its solution. The classical example of the problem has been stated by Wittgenstein is by a metaphor of a fly in a fly-bottle. To show the fly the way out of the fly-bottle is not to illustrate the innumerable directions in which the fly might fly, but to demonstrate the one directions that will take it out of the bottle. Likewise, according to Wittgenstein philosophy does not need to describe the countless uses of a word and statements, but only the one—or once—that will make the problem disappear.

Similarly, the Zen verbalism or the *koan* does not need innumerable interpretations and volumes and a long commentaries to understand its deeper spiritual meanings and significance. However, for solution of the philosophical problem is achieved through the deeper understanding of the language game and insight into the real function of statement under consideration. Likewise, a deeper intellectual intuition is required to understand the real meaning and the mystical significant of Zen Verbalism, because the problems faced by the Zen practitioners and modern philosophers belong to the two different categories. One is spiritual and other is philosophical. However, the solution of both these problems lead to disappearance of the problem. The therapeutic treatment of the problem of the modern thinker would rid one from the misunderstanding of the logic of the language and it would amount in some sense a freedom and the therapeutic solution of the problems of the Zen, practitioner will lead him to *Satori* or freedom.

The Zen Verbalism has no rationalism. The philosophy of Zen Verbalism does not concern with the elucidation of the concept and the riddles, but to liberate the mind from all sorts of rational conceptualization and abstraction. D.T. Suzuki says: "It is no abstraction; it is concrete enough, and direct, as the eye sees — that the sun is, but it is not to be subsumed in the categories of linguistics. As soon as we try to do this, it disappears. The Buddhists, therefore, call it the "unattainable", the "ungraspable."[8]

Zen is a spiritual discipline to attain concrete experience. To express this experience in word or the sentence should not be detached from it. There is an old saying of a Zen-master, "Examine the living words and not the dead ones." The dead words means verbalism which does not communicate directly the concrete experience attained in the state of enlightenment as it is cut off, from the living roots of life. There is "similar practice in both Hindu and Buddhist *Tāntric* traditions. According to the *tāntric* tradition incantation of some form of verbalism known as *Mantra* is required to arouse the dormant divinity which lead to enlightenment. According to the *Tantra* practice only the incantation of living verbalism would bring desired enlightenment, whereas incantation of the dead verbalism which is called *Mantra* without the force of consciousness, would not lead anywhere.[9] The dead words or verbalism says D.T. Suzuki "They have ceased, then, to stir up my being from within, from itself. They are no more what the masters would call "the one word" which when understood leads immediately to the understanding of hundreds of thousands of other words or statements given by the Zen-masters. Zen verbalism deals with these "living words."[10]

The salient feature of Zen Verbalism is that the experience and expression are one. It expresses the most concrete esoteric experience. Zen does not believe in philosophical conceptualization because it does not lead to truth rather it creates philosophical confusion, worse confounded. Its discourse is short, pith and right to the point. The aim of such discourse is to reveal the esoteric structure of the words and sentences which are otherwise clothed in non-sensical verbalism for the laymen. For the Zen practitioners the *koans* or the *mondō* are pregnant with deeper spiritual meaning, the understanding of which lead to *Satori*. Let us examine the following discourse:

"Yakusana (yueh-chan Wei-yan, 750-834) asked Ungan (Yun-yen T'anch'eng, 781-841): "I understand you know how to play with the lion. Am I correct?"

Ungan: "Yes you are right."

Yakusan: "How many lions can you play with?"

Ungan: "Six."

Yakusan: "I also know how to play with the lion."

Ungan: "How many?"

Yakusan: "Just one."

Ungan: "One is six and six is one."

Ungan: Later come to Isan (Kwei-Shan Ling-yu, 771-853) and Isan asked: "I am told that you know how to play with the lion when you were at the Yakusan monastery. Is that right?"

Ungan said: "That is right."

Isan went on: "Do you play with it all the time? Or do you sometimes give it rest?"

Ungan: "If I wish to play with it, I play; if I wish to give it a rest, I give it a rest."

Isan: "When it is at rest, where is it?"

Ungan: "At rest, at rest."[11]

This conversation has a deeper meaning and spiritual significant. Here the lion symbolises senses. The senses are the windows through which we get the impressions. According to Buddhist psychology there are six senses as mind is also considered as a sense, so the six lions symbolise six senses through which we observe the nature. The more we have the organs of the senses we get more dimensions of the world and nature. Though the world of sense perceptions is limited one can think of his space infinitely extended and timeless time. This conversation by Zen-masters to his disciples is the Zen way of communication. It is unique as it believes that the reality is one, concrete, and whole experience, which is called *Satori*. It does not believe in dichotomy of man and nature or subject and object which in Wittgenstein's phrase, "bewitches our intelligence." It is in this state of concrete experience *Śūnyatā* becomes *tathatā*; *tathatā* is *Śūnyatā* and *Śūnyatā* is *tathatā*.

Actional

The actional method of experiencing enlightenment is a process of realization of the pervasive and universal nature of reality; *tathatā* or suchness through concrete experience. Goso-Hoyen a Zen-master of the Śuṅga dynasty reveals the Zen experience in the following way. He says that, if someone ask me to explain Zen I would say that, it is like learning the art of burglary. He tries to explain the Zen through a parables. There was a burglar. When his son saw him becoming very old he thought of learning the art of burglary from his father, because he thought after father's death he would not be able to provide bread to his family members if he would not know the trade secret. He requested his father for the transmission of the art of burglary. In one dark night the father took the son to a rich man's bungalow. He entered the house after breaking the fences and opened a large chest. After taking out the clothing from the chest, father asked the son to go in. The moment the son went inside the chest father dropped the lid and locked it. The father came out of the bungalow and knocked at the door and got the inmates of the house awakened and he slipped away, quietly. The inmates of the house after seeing the holes in the fence created by burglar started searching the burglars with lamps. The son of the burglar was confined in the chest and he was cursing his cruel father. In the moment of deep anguish and excitement an idea flashed in his mind. He started making a noise like the gnawing of a rat. The owner of the house asked one of the maid servant to search the chest with the lamp. The moment the maid opened the chest, the burglar's son came out blowing out the light and elbowing the maid fled away. The people started chasing him. He saw a well by the side of the road and pick up a large stone and threw it into the water. The owner of the house and his men who were chasing the burglar's son; thought, that the thief fell into the well, and all of them gathered round the well trying to find burglar drowning himself in the dark hole, by dozing the owner of the house and his man. In the meantime burglar's son reached his home safely. After reaching home he started scolding his father for his providential escape. Father maintaining his mental equanimity and asked his son, not to be offended and requested him to narrate the whole story of his getting out from the chest and reaching to the home. After hearing all about the adventure of his son the old burglar said to his son, "There you are my son you have learn the art."[12]

In the ancient Hindu Upaniṣadic tradition, there are similar parables. There was a lion and lioness living in a jungle. One day the cub of lion was lost. It was picked up by shepherd. He reared the cub along with sheep. When the cub was grown up he started behaving like a sheep. One day when the lion went out for a hunting he joined his lost cub behaving like a sheep. After seeing the lion cub was also frightened like other sheep and ran for life along with them. The lion caught hold the cub and started convincing him that he was also a lion like him and not a sheep. But no amount of argument, intellectual persuasion would convince the cub that he was a lion not a sheep. Then the lion took him to nearby pond and pointing out towards the similar reflections of both of them, said, that, you could see now that you were like me and not like sheep and he roared, and he asked him also to roar. The cub roared and he had the realization that, he was a lion which he was always.

The idea behind these stories is to demonstrate the futility of conceptualization and verbal instructions we cannot attain liberation because bondage is creation of our own intellectual ignorance. Both the Hindu and Buddhist traditions point out that enlightenment or

Satori cannot be attained through scriptural learning and philosophical debate. It is an act of concrete experience which grows out of one's own inner light. This experience is to be lived, not to be conceptualized.

Rinzai Zen and *Sōtō* Zen

During the time of Hui-Neng, the sixth patriarch of China chism occurred in Zen Buddhism. The concept of enlightenment and its technique became the point of philosophical disputation and disagreement which led to the split of Zen Buddhism into two prominent sects, known as *Rinzai* and *Sōtō* Schools. The *Rinzai* School believes that the true wisdom (*Bodhi-njñāna*) is undifferentiated and spontaneous. On the other hand the *Sōtō* School emphases the gradual realization of enlightenment.

Hui-Neng was a lay-peddler. He was not a man of scholastic background according to historical account available to us. His initial inspiration to become Zen came from *Vajrachedikā Sūtra* as the story goes when Hui-Neng paddling wood he overheard, the recitation of *Vajrachedikā Sūtra*. This proved to be the turning point of his life of uncouth paddler. He decided to study Zen Buddhism under Hung-Jen, the fifth patriarch. After joining the Zen monastery he worked in the granary as a rice-cleaner and remained there for eight months. In the meantime Hung-Jen thought of transmission of his knowledge and spiritual power to his successor. A search for the same started among his five hundred disciples (monks). Shen-Shiu was a most powerful contender for the successorship, because, he was well-versed in scriptural knowledge. Improved of his superior scholastic knowledge and erudition he composed the following poems:

> "This body is the Bodhi-trees,
> The soul is like a mirror bright;
> Take heed to keep it always clean,
> And let not dust collect upon it."

Hui-Neng surprised everybody by his following inscriptions beside the Shen-Shiu's poem:

> "The Bodhi-tree is not like the tree,
> The mirror bright is nowhere shining;

As there is nothing from the beginning,
Where can the dust collect itself?"

The above two poems epitomize the two distinct traditions of Buddhism. The Hui-Neng's poem speaks of the philosophy of *Prajñāpāramitā* and *Vajrachedikā*, it is in tune with the doctrine of *Śūnyatā* of *Mahāyāna* Buddhism, whereas Shen-Shiu's poem speaks of great erudition and scholastic understanding of the *sūtra*. The two differ on the nature and technique of *Satori*. Hui-Neng would emphasise on the spontaneity of *Satori* and his school was known as *Tun-chiao*, which means spontaneous teaching, in contradiction to *Shen-shiu's Chien-Chieo* which means gradual teaching. The former became very popular in south and later in the north and this geographical demarcation became the reason for the name of new two sects known as Southern School (*Nantsung*) and Northern School (*Pe-tsuing*).

There are two methods of acquiring knowledge, i.e. reason and intuition. The religious teachers have preference for intuition as they believe that reality is beyond the reach of reason whereas scholastic teachers have preference for reason. This initial emphasis on the nature of *Satori* and respective value of the scholasticism led down the foundation of two sects of Zen Buddhism which is known as *Sōtō* Zen and *Rinzai* Zen. D.T. Suzuki says that the Northern School tended to value learning and practical discipline, while the Southern School strongly uphold the intuitive functioning of *prajñā,* which takes place spontaneously that is immediately without resorting to logical process.[13]

The war of supremacy and authenticity started between the southern school of *Hui-neng* and northern school of *Shen-shiu* and later with the quietist movement of some of the Zen-masters the Śuṅga Dynasty in this war of succession *Hui-neng* became victorious and was declared as the sixth patriarch. Buddhism was made rooted in Chinese culture and life and undergone great change and metamorphosis. The *Hui-neng* did not attach any importance to the scriptural studies and Zazen (quite sitting) as some Zen-masters. There is a conceptual difference between Shen-shiu and Hui-neng conception of Buddha-mind. According to Shen-shiu Buddhahood is the essence of one's being. One can attain enlightenment if one remains unpolluted by the dust of lust and anger, sex and hunger. Shen-shiu says: mind is like a mirror which is blurred by the dust of passion. If we keep our mind from the contamination of passion we will attain Buddhahood which we are essentially. On the contrary Hui-neng holds that the dust wiping school of Shen-shiu speaks of dualistic nature of reality, which is not. To say dust and mind is to believe in the duality of reality whereas nothing is neither dust nor mind and which is called in *Mahāyāna* Buddhism no mind. There is a state of suchness *tathatā* and Zen is nothing but a finger pointing to the way.

Hui-neng's *gāthā* which made him the sixth patriarch is full of riddles and enigma which a few can understand and fewer can resolve. Hui-neng's preference to intuition than the reason attracted masses, because, intuition is not the sole possession of scholastic being.

The *Rinzai* school introduced a new technique for the attainment of *Satori*. The *Rinzai* School believes that to create the overwhelming feeling of doubt is necessary for creating the esoteric conditions for dawn of new wisdom. This new technique is known as *Koan*. Alan Watts holds the view that "intensity or the *Satori* is proportionate to the intensity of the feeling of doubt."[14] The *Sōtō* school does not give much religious importance to the *Koan* system whereas the *Rinzai* school considers it as necessary condition for the attainment of *Satori*. *Sōtō* school believes the *Koan* system is an artificial devise to awaken *Bodhijñāna*. It further argues that the *Satori* attained by *Koan* would be fake *Satori*, because of its dualistic character. This school is of the opinion that *Satori* can be attained through proper *Dhyāna* alone. We are of the opinion that the *Satori* attained through the system of *Koan* would not be an artificial *Satori*. *Satori* is a direct, integral, immediate and total comprehension of suchness. *Satori* which does not characterize the above conditions and nature is not a *Satori*. There cannot be real and artificial *Satori*. We shall discuss in greater detail the distinction between *Satori* and knowledge senselessness and dreamless sleep and awaking state in the fourth Chapter. We also do not agree with Alan W. Watts's view as there is no correlation with psychological or otherwise between the intensity of doubt and the intensity of *Satori* experience. *Satori* experience, logically speaking is no experience.

The *Sōtō* School adopts the practice of *Shikan-taza* for the attainment of *Satori*. *Shikan* means "nothing but" or "just" while *ta* means "to hit" and *Za* "to sit." Hence, the practice of *Shikan-taza* is different from spontaneous method of *Koan* and *Mondō* practice of

Rinzai school which concentrate on *prajñā* for sudden illumination. The practice of *Shikah-taza* may be compared with the *Upaniṣadic* conception of treading the path of spirituality as walking on the razor's edge. The Chinese Zen-master belonging to the *Sōtō*-school compares the mental equilibrium attains through the practice of *Shikan-taza* with a sword's man facing the death during the duel. A swordsman engaged in the duel of Swordsmanship remains ever watchful and vigilance because the slightest relaxation on the part of swordsman would cause his life during the fight a crowd watches in interest with every movement of the fight swordsman also sees from the corner of his eyes and bears the voice of applause, and jeering of the crowd, but never for a moment give vein to his sense impression. This mental equipoise and equilibrium is necessary both for the swords man while fighting against his enemy and the Zen practitioner fighting against the lure of sex and hunger and love and anger. The practice of *Shikan-taza* heighten the state of consciousness in which one is neither tense nor hurry and remains unconcern.

This state of Zen consciousness and mental integration is known as state of *Daigi* (fixation). This state of oneness or *ekagratā* is called *Agrayā-buddhi* in *Upaniṣadic* tradition through which one attains enlightenment.

On the other hand *Rinzai* school believes that the practice of *Shikan-taza* does not bring illumination unless it is wedded to *prajñā*. This integration of *prajñā* and *Upāya, Śūnyatā* and *Karuṇā* brings sudden illumination. The illumination has been used in a different connotations. Here sudden illumination according to *Rinzai* sect is "Seeing" things and beings as they are, that is in their state of suchness. This suchness constitutes the essence of mind in which all distinctions between particulars are dissolved into nothingness. There is a famous sayings of *Hui-neng* that "all distinctions are falsely imaginations." In contradiction to *Sōtō* school thought the *Rinzai* school considers the achievement of no-mind which is always spontaneous and sudden, as the central objective of Zen's practice which is rooted in everyday life and not confined to the four walls of monastic living.

This down to earth philosophy of Zen Buddhism captured the imagination of Japanese people and it has taken a firm root in the culture and the tradition of them. *Eisai* and *Dōgen* are the two outstanding Zen-masters who after undergoing the intense training and attaining wisdom and knowledge in China they founded the two schools of thought, namely *Rinzai* and *Sōtō*. These two founding fathers of Zen Buddhism were greatest Zen-master that Japan have produced. *Eisai* (1141-1215) the Japanese *I'ient-ai* monk propagated and popularized *Rinzai Zen* thought with imperial support and established monasteries at *Kyōto* and *Kamakura*. The *Rinzai* Zen came to Japan shortly after the beginning of the *Kamakura* era when the military dictators *Yoritomo* and with the support of his *Samurai* class captured the political and the military power from the hand of nobility. The cultural and the religious life was in a state of schism and disintegration, and a great void was created. Arrival of *Rinzai* Zen captured the imagination of the *Samurai* class (military class), because of its down to earth philosophical approach of life and its simple and direct approach to religious experience, which gave birth to a new philosophy known as *Boshido*. *Boshido* means the Tao of warrior which has emerged from the impact of Zen thought to the arts of war.

The conversion of the *Samurai* class into *Rinzai* Zen Buddhism created puzzlement for many Buddhist scholars and cultural anthropologists. *Rinzai* Zen neutral stand on moral virtue was one of the reason for the acceptance of this school of thought to *Samurai* class.

The *Sōtō* school was established in Japan in A.D. 1227 by a great Zen-master Dōgen (A.D. 1200-1263). He established the great monastery of Eihieji, refusing the imperial patronage. Dōgen received his initial training from Eisai from the founder of the *Rinzai* School. Dōgen was ceased with the philosophical problems created by the teachings of Buddhism. According to *Mahāyāna* Buddhism our essential nature is *Bodhi,* but we have to strive for enlightenment. Eisai's answer instead of satisfying Dōgen mind it provoked him. After the death of Eisai Dōgen the eldest spent eight years with Myōzen the eldest disciple of Eisai and resolved some *Koans* and received initiation. This attainment of enlightenment could not satisfied the questioning mind of Dōgen and he undertook a long and difficult pilgrimage to China in search of peace and total illumination. After the practice of *Shikan-taza* he attained the great enlightenment under loving care of Nyōzo at the famous Tient-tung monastery of China. The *Shikantaza* became the central concept of *Sōtō* school. The *Sōtō* school became very popular amongst the Japanese masses because of the practice of *Shikan-tanza*.

In our opinion there is no much conceptual difference between the *Rinzai* and the *Sōtō* school of thought. The apparent difference is due to the respective emphasis given by these two schools on the emphasis and nature of *Satori*. There are different stages of *Satori* both in *Mahāyāna* and *Theravāda* traditions. According to *Theravāda* Buddhism *Sōtapatti* (stream-winner), *Sakadāgāmi* (one-returner), *An āgāmi* (non-returner) and *Arhat* (enlightened-being) for the stages of *Nirvāṇa* (*Satori*). The *Upaniṣadic* tradition particularly the *Yōga* system also believes in the different and gradual stages of *Samādhī* known as *Samprajñāta* and *Asamprajñāta*. There is a gradual ascent to consciousness and the attainment of different stages of *Satori*. But each stage is attained spontaneously and this Zen experience is total, and undifferentiated. Zen-master Soyen Shaku, the teacher of Dr. D.T. Suzuki is also of the view that these two schools of thought originated from *Sheu-hsiu* and *Hui-neng* are the wings of a bird, the two wheels of a cart or, perhaps more exactly one is like the eye and the other the legs'.[15]

Notes

1. *Yoga* (Mircea Eliade) translated from the French by Willord R. Trask, Bollingen Series, LVI, Princeton University Press, 2nd Edn. (1969), p. 169.
2. *The New Encyclopaedia Britannica*, Vol. 3 by Encyclopaedia Britannica Inc. (1975), U.S.A., p. 386.
3. *Encyclopaedia of Buddhism*, Vol. III, by G.P. Malalasekera, (1972), Published by the Government of Sri Lanka, Government Press, Ceylon, p. 194.
4. *Ibid.*, Vol. III., pp. 194-95.
5. *Encyclopaedia of Religion and Ethics*, Vol. IV, p. 703.
6. *Tractatus*, 6.522 (p. 151).
7. *Indian Philosophy*, Vol. I, pp. 682-83.
8. D.T. Suzuki, *Zen and Japanese Culture*, London: Routledge and Kegan Paul, (1959), p. 7.
9. *Kulārṇava Tantra*, Chapter 15, Verse 61, p. 336, Madras: Ganesh & Co., (1965).
10. *Zen and Japanese Culture*, *op. cit.*, pp. 7-8.
11. *The Transmission of the Lamp*, Fas. XIV (Refer with, Zen and Japanese Culture, by D.T. Suzuki).
12. *The Savings of Goso Hoyen* (Refer with, Zen and Japanese Culture, by D.T. Suzuki).
13. *Essays in Zen Buddhism*, Buddhist Society, London, Rides & Company, (1950), p. 43 (by D.T. Suzuki).
14. *Way of Zen* (by Alen W. Watts), Third Edition (D.T. Suzuki), New York, (1958), Pantheon, U.S.A., p. 107.
15. *Zen: A Way of Life*, p. 89.

CHAPTER 4
The Concept of Koan

The *Koan* and the Limitation of Thought

The derivative meaning of the *Koan* in original Chinese language is a case which establishes the legal precedent. In Chinese it is pronounced as *kung-an,* and in Japanese *ko-an*. However, this word has been used in Zen Buddhism as a formulation and a riddle pointing to the experience of awakening. The language has its own limitation, realizing the limitation of expressing the inexplicable Wittgenstein discarded the isomorphic relation between language and reality. Language is a symbol. We have been developing different symbols (languages) to express the different levels of our experience. B. Russell and Whitehead after realizing the inadequacy of the prevalent language in expressing the mathematical formulations and theories they developed a new language known as symbolic logic. Likewise, the ancient Indian thinkers especially Kabir and *Siddhācārya* of *Sahajiya* sect of Bengal expressed themselves in language which is known as *Sandhyā-bhāṣā* to describe the philosophical truth and mystic experience. The utterances of Kabir and the *Siddhācārya*'s are nothing but non-sensical statements for the lay-men, but for a man of spiritual insight and vision these utterances are pregnant with deeper philosophical import.

The contemporary mind is engaged in the determining the conditions and limits of what is sayable and what is unsayable. The investigations into the logical structure of thought and knowledge led to believe that which can be thought can be given linguistic expression. We cannot deny the existence on the basis of our empirical investigation; to deny the existence of something on the basis of language would amount to say off, what cannot be said. The analysis of the logical structure of thought in a language led him

(Wittgenstein) to introduce the concept of mystical which is the integral part of his philosophy. Wittgenstein says: that "propositions can express nothing of what is higher."[1] It means that the mystical is that which would be non-sensical to discuss, describe or even to think, because, it lies beyond the limit of language. The structure and the function of language has been so designed that it can be said what is sayable and it cannot be said what is unsayable. It means the mystical is an experience which can be revealed and felt but cannot be put into words.

The introduction of *Koan* in Buddhism is not a new device or a technique to throw the mind of its familiar way of logical reasoning to start the process of emptying it from all sorts of metapsychosis which was prevalent practice in ancient India. The mystical experience transcends logic and common sense and hence it cannot be expressed in ordinary language. This is why the Indian mystic and Zen-masters did not use any statement to transmit their teachings rather they used carefully divice so called non-sensical riddles known as *Koan*s to point out in the words of Ikbal; there is a world beyond the stars and the trial of mystical love is still ahead.[2] One of the popular Zen saying is that; when some elder point out with his finger towards a moon to some children, the children sometime identified the finger with the moon and he did not comprehend the moon. So most of us identify ourselves with non-self-known as *pañcakkhanda* (five aggregates), i.e. *Rūpa* (coporiality), *Vedanā* (feeling), *Saṁjñā* (perception), *Saṁskāra* (mental formation) and *Vijñāna* (consciousness) and fall to comprehend "I" as en extension of *tathatā* or suchness. Everything is reality. There is not a speck of dust outside the realm of *Buddha*-mind, which the Zen-masters call cosmic mind. No scission exists between the material world and that of pure essence in the words of *Nāgārjuna*. There is no difference between *Nirvāṇa* and *Saṁsāra*; *Nirvāṇa* is *Saṁsāra* and *Saṁsāra* is *Nirvāṇa*. The use of *Koan* is to solve the riddle of "I" and the world, *Nirvāṇa* and *Saṁsāra*. With the practice of *Koan* mind undergoes complete metamorphosis. It is an act of integration of *Nirvāṇa* and *Saṁsāra* that can never be described nor thought. So long we live in the world of dualism we play what Wittgenstein calls language game. But when after practising *Koan* once enters into the world of *Satori*, one becomes free from identification with superficial reality. "The complete solution of a *Koan* involves the movement of the mind from a state of ignorance (delusion) to the vibrant inner awareness of living truth. This implies the emergence into the field of consciousness of the immaculate Bodhi-mind, which is the reverse of the mind of delusion."[3]

The *Koan* is a statement of Roshi Zen-master to unfold the Zen psychology in the mind of the lay practitioner. The understanding of the *Koan* leads to the state of consciousness of which the *Koan* is an expression. When the *Koan* is understood mind becomes free from conceptualizations and abstractions. This state of consciousness is *Satori*.

In the beginning of almost all the mystic history, the master used to examine the mental and the moral state of a pupil by question and answer session with the sole objective of giving aids to the pupil in proper understanding the real nature of truth. The philosophical puzzlement and perplexity created in the mind of the pupil paves the path for searching and contriving. In the mystic tradition of all religions the master would have to wait for a long time for the pupils' first question. The first question mirrors the inner crisis with which the pupil is ceased, which is the harbinger of dawn of a new light and a new wisdom. The great teacher is he, who creates a crisis in the pupil's mind and get out of it successfully. This awakens the inner being and leads him to reality. The practicing of *Koan* is outcome of the ancient mystic traditions of question and answer session between master and pupils. This question and answer session which is called *mondō* in Japanese attracted the logical mind of the West and attempt was being made consistently for intellectual comprehension or interpretation of the *Koan*. The elucidation and the clarification of *Koan* proved furtile. The greatest detrimental factors in resolving the *Koan* is the intellect which discriminates subject and object. This discriminating function of intellect creates delusion which is called *Māyā* in Hindu philosophy. This delusion erroneously identifies man with different objects which is bondage. Under spell of this delusion man weaves a cobweb to get himself encaged in it. This seals man real consciousness. To unlock the encaged being and lead him into awakening, into the state of *Satori*, is the purpose behind the puzzlement and perplexity created by *Koan*. D.T. Suzuki says: "an examination we at once notice that there is no room in the *Koan* to insert an intellectual interpretation. The knife is not sharp enough to cut the *Koan* open and see what are its contents. For a *Koan* is not a logical proposition but the expression of a certain mental state resulting from the Zen discipline."[4]

We are giving few illustrations of *Koan*:

Question – 1 When amon Chao-chou "what is the meaning of the first patriarch visits to China."

Chau-Chou: The cypress tree is the front of court-yard.

Question – 2 Monk: Is there the Buddha-nature in a dog.

Chau-Chou: "Wu" (mu in Japanese).

Question – 3 Monk: "All things are said to be reducible to the ONE, but where is the one to be reduced?"

Chou Chou: "When I was in the distress of Ching's I had a robe made that weighed seven chin."

Question – 4 When Chou-Chou went to study Zen under Man Ch'saun be put a question, "What is the Tao"?

Answer: "Noua-Chiswen your everyday mind, that is the Tao."

Question – 5 Monk – "Who is Buddha"?

Answer: Tung-Shan, Zen-master: "Three Chin of flax."

If we examine the above statements then we do not find any relation between first patriarch visit to China and cypress tree, Buddha-nature and Wu, all things said to be reducible into one and the robe of Chou chou's weight seven chin; we cannot find out any logical coherence. For the layman the above dialogues between the Zen-masters and their pupils bear no philosophical truth. The above statements from positivistic point of view are senseless, utterances, but from mystical point of view the above statements are pregnant with deep esoteric meaning. All our experience are not noetic and all our experiences cannot be put into linguistic form. All our enquiries cannot be answer. The above answers of the Zen-masters are in conformity with the Buddhistic tradition. Lord Buddha also did not answer many questions and preferred to remain silence. His silence generated philosophical disputations and argumentations which enriched the Buddhist philosophy and gave rise to many sects and philosophical schools. What we would like to emphasize here that above questions of the Zen practitioners may not come under the strict category of *Avyaktāni* (unanswerable questions), but answers of Zen-masters are pointers to the answerable nature of their enquiries. In accordance with Śākyamuni stands taken on such problems the Zen-masters simply want to emphasize the meaningless of metaphysical enquiries. The ultimate truth of life cannot be conceptualized, but it is to be lived and experienced. In the verbal disputations and philosophical speculations create the intellectual dust which blind the real vision of man. For the realization of reality the practice of *Dhyāna* is must and not the indulgence in logical deputations and argumentations. *Koan* is a mystic device to expose the meaninglessness of philosophical polemic and point out that greatest truth of life lies beyond the reach of reason and senses.

Koan as a means to transcend the limit of Thought

Zen Buddhism is neither a doctrine nor a philosophical speculation. It is an experience pregnant with deeper meaning and truth. This experience validates its own authority. It does not need any support from the scripture nor from dialectical process of reasoning. It is realization of ultimate truth and being which is born out of the direct experience of *tathatā*. It does not take even the teaching of the Buddha and Zen-masters seriously until the truth is assimilated into his own being, and it becomes one's own living experience. This experience transcends both the sense and the reason. The Zen-masters have developed the technique to communicate this experience into a verbal form and this is known as *Koan*. *Koan* is an expression of the Zen experience in its uncouth and incomprehensive way.

The very nature and the content of Zen experience warrants its utterances in form of *Koan* because it springs from one's own inner being. It is like the blossoming of flower in the spring. To understand the nature and the content of the Zen experience one will have to go through the rigour of *Koan* practice. This is why Zen-masters avoid verbal explanation or elucidation of this experience, because this experience is not a concept but whole-truth. The mind does not have the capabilities to comprehend this whole-truth. This experience of enlightenment has been beautifully explained through the help of metaphor, by Swami Ramakrishna. Swami Ramakrishna says that, "to measure the depth and the intensity of the spiritual experience is like measuring the fathom of the ocean by the doll of salt. The moment the salt-doll goes to fathom, the depth of the ocean it loses its own identity, but by losing its own identity it becomes the ocean." This is the process of spiritualization of man. It is the process of becoming. The *Koan* is not an intellectual mediation but it is uncouth experience of truth that pervades the whole cosmos. It is spiritual transformation of mind from the state of delusion to the state of inner living awareness of whole-truth. This transformation of one's own being gives a rise to the emergence of new consciousness of Bodhi mind. Crippling with the *Koan* generates faith and confidence in the reality of Bodhi mind. The purpose of the *Koan* practice is to liberate the mind free from the snare of subjectivity. The enigmatic nature and the structure of *Koan* has been designed to blind our external eyes by kicking dust, so that one can see and realize the truth as it is.

The Zen-masters have selected the subject matter of *Koans* from day-to-day experience of our life such as a dog, a tree, a horse, a finger and thereby, they give value and importance to the empirical reality and thereby stop the mind in getting engaged in useless abstractions of concepts. The *Koan*s are the expressions of living truth which is one interdependent whole. The experience of the whole certify that there is no difference between *saṁsāra* end *nirvāṇa.* The *saṁsāra* and the *nirvāṇa* constitute the whole truth. The *Koan* depicts the limitation of thought and the reason. Philip Kapleans says: "The Chinese Zen-masters, those spiritual geniuses who created these paradoxical dialogues, did not hesitate to thumb their noses at logic and common sense in their marvellous creations. By wheedling the intellect into attempting solutions impossible for it, *Koan*s reveal to us the inherent limitations of the logical mind as an instrument for realizing ultimate Truth."[5]

The practice of the *Koan* is aimed at to stir the mind of all feelings, emotions and passions which delude the mind. By stirring the mind from the passions and emotions one gets oneself established in his own true being. This is purpose behind the yoga practice.[6] In Hindu psychology it is said that the truth or the true being is covered with five *Kośas* sheaths, namely, *Kāmamaya Kośa*, *Manōmaya Kośa, Atimānasa Kośa*, *Vijñānamaya Kośa* and *Hiraṇyamaya Kośa.* With the progress in spirituality one gets strip of from these *kośas* one by one and enters into the world of reality. This experience of reality is called *Samādhi*. The stripping of the different *kośas* means the getting rid from the passions and the emotions. Lu K'uan Yu rightly observed that, "The aim of the Ch'an sect is to strip the mind of all feelings and passions for the purpose of disentangling it from the phenomenal so that the self-nature can return to its normal state and operate in the normal way without hindrance.[7] The purpose of the *Koan* practice is to rid oneself from the beliefs and prejudices from the discriminating knowledge of good and bad, and to shed the false notions of self and none-self so that one can have the peep into the world of perfection which is in fact not different from our day-to-day experience of pain and pleasure. The enlightenment integrates the self to non-self, the pain with pleasure, world with *nirvāṇa,* because the feeling of differentiation is bondage, and the experience of oneness in enlightenment. It is the impurities which deludes the mind. Impurities are false thinking. The object of *Koan* practice is to prepare the mind for the experience of the Buddha-nature. Buddha-nature is the quintessence of one's own being and existence. But due to our delusion and false thinking we are unable to have the experience of our true being. It is through the *Koan* practice that one can eradicate one's false thinking and get into reality.

Zen Buddhism became a living cult in China since its introduction by *Bodhidharma* after his arrival in China until after the passing of the Hui-neng the sixth patriarch it was accepted as a way of life because of its down to earth approach to reality. The introduction of the *Koan* and its impact on the spiritual and moral life heralded a new era of religious renaissance. It discovered a new ground for the realization. The religious life of the then China was engaged in the practice of lifeless dogmas and rituals. The introduction of Zen Buddhism by its first Chinese patriarch came as a rescue, for those who have genuinely interested in getting enlightenment and it caught the imagination of both the monks and lay-men and a new era of spiritual regeneration was usher in. This school of thought particularly the practice of *Koan* led emphasis on the inability of mind and senses in comprehending the reality that is Bodhi-mind. The *Koan* practice became very popular because of its directness. It appeals the deepest psyche of man and it arouses the inner being which constitute the *Bodhi*-mind. Without the realization of this inner being or *Bodhi*-mind a man is a less than a man. The radical approach of Zen Buddhism exposed the hollowness of the ritualistic religion. According to Zen Buddhism religion is realization. It is an experience of *Satori.* If the religion does not serve this purpose it is anything but religion. This experience transcends the limitation of our thought and mind. The practice of *Koan* teach the method to transcend the limitation of thought, so that one can enter into the world of reality.

The emergence of the *Koan* practice was a natural growth in the history of Zen Buddhism. The function of *Koan* is to recreate esoteric condition for the emergence of Zen experience. The practice of the *Koan* resulted in making the mind one-pointedness which is in common parlance is called meditative ideation. In Hindu *yoga* system it is called *Agrayā-Buddhi.* When mind is made one pointed it attains *Satori.* The scientific explanation of using this technique of concentration and meditation is to dissolve the mind into the ocean of consciousness. The property of mind is to remain in the state of flux and change and hence if it is made to concentrate through the practice of *Koan* it would go out of its existence. Method of meditation is applied universally in all the mystic sects of the world, becomes enlightenment can be achieved only by transcending the limitation of thought. The state of the awakening is the state of thoughtlessness and nothingness (WU). The practice of *Koan* is a process of emptying the mind.

The practice of *Koan* is intimately related to the practice *Nembutsu. Nembutsu* is an esoteric technique to incontate the *Bīja-mantra* of *Amita-Buddha.* This practice of *Nembutsu* can be traced to the whole lotus society founded by *Hui-yuan* (died 416). According to D.T. Suzuki the Chinese Buddhism was developed along the two traditions of Zen and *Nembutsu.* However, both the Zen and *Nembutsu* were closely related with the esoteric practice and both the school of thought believed that enlightenment can be attained through the esoteric practice.

Koan practice is based on the principle that knowledge acquired through sense and intellect, does not reveal the real nature of the thing and being. All discursive knowledge gives the differential view of the world. The true knowledge springs out of one's own being. The *Koan* practice awakens the inner being and offers a vistas of a new world of consciousness. This state of spiritual awareness is achieved through the rigours and the severe disciplining of mind. Each one of us is a Buddha. It is a question of realization. This realization can come through the practice of *Koan* which cut asunder, the trammels of delusion. The technique of *Koan* practice is a methodology of transcending the limit of thought, so that, one can awaken his inner being. This awakening is *Satori.*

The *Koan* and the *Mondō*

The *Koan* and the *Mondō* are unique concepts of Zen Buddhism. The *Koan* and the *Mondō* are based on Buddhist esotericism. *Mondō* is popularly known as question and answer session between the Zen-masters and their disciples. This unique dialogue between master and student is aimed at awakening the deeper levels of disciple's intuitive mind Disciple, perplexed by philosophical problems, seeks clarifications from the master.

The subjects of the *Mondō* are vast and varied. For the layman these *mondōs* appear to be enigmatic and sometimes non-sensical, but for the initiates these *mondōs* are pregnant with philosophical and esoteric significance. According to Zen Buddhism there is no other method more effective than the *mondō* to arouse the *prajñā* which leads one to *nirvāṇa*. This Zen methodology became very popular since the very inception of Zen Buddhism. There is conceptual difference between the *mondō* and the dialogue. The very nature of dialogue is to destroy the simple faith by depicting the opposite of the truth believed to be true. The purpose of the dialogue is to destroy the very foundation of monolithic character of the truth. The beauty of the dialogue is that the seed of a new truth is sown in the process of its destruction. The first stage of dialectical reasoning leads to scepticism and denial. In the subsequent process of dialectical reasoning the truth of being becomes the truth of becoming, and thus this endless process continues which proves that the ultimate truth is beyond the reach of dialectical reasoning.

In the early stage of Zen Buddhism disciple used to come with problem to the master. The problem was in a way index of the mental state of the disciple. The master used to wait for a long time for the disciples first question. The question was a proof of disciple's spiritual crisis. The disciple put question to the master for its solution only when the disciple was faced with puzzlement and perplexity. The master used to accelerate the intensity of the spiritual crisis through the methodology of *mondō* with a view to rid the mind of nuisance (*avidyā*). For the dawn of enlightenment the mental crisis and the puzzlement is necessary. Even the Buddha had to go through this process of perplexity and puzzlement. According to Buddhist mythology when *Siddhārtha* saw sick man, the old man, and the dead-body, he was faced with the philosophical crisis and in the process of its solution he attained *nirvāṇa* and he enumerated the four noble truths which became the corner stones of Buddhist religion and philosophy. There is a story about Swāmī Rāmakrishna Paramahan. One of the disciple of Swāmi Rāmakrishna asked question from him that why he was not having God realization. Swāmī Rāmakrishna asked him to see him the following morning at bank of river where, his *Āśrama* was situated? The disciple came to see Swāmījī who was taking bath in the river. Swāmījī asked the disciple to follow him. When the disciple came nearer to Swāmījī he asked him to take dip in the water. When the disciple took the dip in the water Swāmījī pressed his head below the water for few moments and after that he relieved him. When he came out of the water the disciple was in a state of puzzlement and the disciple asked Swāmījī, why he did so? If he would not have been relieved he would have died. Swāmījī said this is the answer of your question. He said, if you would have the same intense feeling for God realization then only you will attain liberation. Likewise in the Zen Buddhist tradition the question is a pointer that the disciple is faced with the puzzlement and the crisis and the ground has been prepared for the sprout of the spiritual seedlings. The *Mondō* is an esoteric method to wipe out the mind from all traces of *metempsychosis*, or mental formation (*saṁskāra*), so that, master can enkindle the light of *Satori*; that is there in every man. The master is conversant with the process to lead the disciple to a crisis and get him out of it successfully. This was the beginning of the *Koan* exercise.

There is an intimate relation between the *Koan* and the *Mondō*. The *Koan* is a word or a phrase which does not convey any intellectual meaning. Such as "Has a dog Buddha-nature?" or "What is the sound of one hand clapping?" This method is applied to keep the disciple engaged in solving the problems which are intellectually insolvable. The disciple is ceased with the problem and he tries to understand the *Koans*. More the disciple tries to solve the *Koan* the more enigmatic it becomes and as a result the tension grows and the disciple has to spend sleepless nights for weeks and months. The master watches the disciple and he comes for the spiritual help at the right moment. The practice of the *Koan* involves a great danger, like the practice of *tantra-yoga*. The practice of *Koan* and the *tantra-yoga* is done under the supervision of a teacher of a very high order. Christians Humphreys says, that: "But the *Koan* system has its dangers. In the absence of a highly qualified and trained Rōshi to assist the pupil there is no one to say when he is on or off the beam in his endeavours, and none to say when he has genuinely solved his *Koan*. More important, there is no one to protect his from raising such a head of steam as one student calls it, that without very experienced guidance the whole mind may crack, meaning temporary or permanent insanity."[8]

The practice of the *Koan* and the *Mondō* is to help the pupils in breaking the barriers of various thoughts and to awaken one's *prajñā* (intuition) by meditating for weeks and months in crossed legs posture. Meditation without proper instructions and guidance would lead nowhere. One Rōshi once saw his disciple engaged in meditation for the whole day, but he could see that, the disciple was practicing meditation without proper instruction and as such he was not making any progress. He asked, "what are you seeking in this way?" "The disciple answered, to become the Buddha." The master, picked up, a piece of brick and started polishing it on stone. The disciple enquired from the master, "what are you doing Sir?" The master replied "making a mirror."

Disciple : "You want make a mirror by polishing a brick."
Master : "And no amount of sitting crossed legged will make you Buddha."

This whole *Mondō* is aimed at imparting proper instructions on the esoteric aspect of meditation. The meditation practice under the proper esoteric guidance gives the desirable results, that is the awakening of the *prajñā* and this is why, master in the end of the question and answer session says, "It is like driving a cart when it would not move, do you whip the cart or the ox?" What master wants to convey is very simple truth. The practice of Zen Buddhism is related to the awakening of *prajñā* what is called in Buddhist *tantra.* The dormant divinity (*Heruka*); and Hindu Tantra it is called awakening of *Kuṇḍalinī Śakti*. Here the cart symbolises the physical body and the ox stands for the *prajñā*. The aim of the Zen practice is to awaken the *prajñā* and hence sitting in cross-legged postures for day and night would not help unless it is directed against the awakening of the *prajñā* or what is called primary man. Kabir also illustrates the same point of view by giving another example of the practice of *Yōga* without spiritual goal or guidance. He says, like the above Zen-masters, the practice of meditation without meditative insight and incantation is like the movement of ox engaged in crashing the oil seeds which goes on moving and moving round the oil crusher but it does not make any progress. D.T. Suzuki rightly observes: "The problem of *prajñā* which constitutes the essence of Buddhist philosophy is really in exhaustible, and no amount of talk seems to suffice. I will give some more *mondō* here and indicate the trend of thought underlying them. Until the relation between *Vijñāna* and *Prajñā*, or that between *prajñā*-intuition and *Vijñāna*-reasoning, is thoroughly understood, such ideas as *Śūnyatā* (emptiness), *tathatā* (suchness), *mōkṣa* (emancipation), *nirvāṇa* and others will not be fully absorbed as living ideas."[9]

The Zen Buddhism aims at releasing the inner tension produced by the experience of mental duality. Unless and until the inner crisis is heightened no approach to Zen-master would be fruitful. There is no scriptures on Zen Buddhism. However, the Zen Buddhism derives philosophical and esoteric inspiration from the *Yōgācāra* school and *Prajñāpāramitā sutta*. The concept of *Śūnyatā* and *tathatā* provides the doctrinal basis of Zen Buddhism. The *Koan* and the *mondō* are not the end of Zen rather they are the beginning of the final path which nobody else, but the seeker of the truth will have to tread. "I am the way", said Jesus, "I am *Brahma*, I am *Ātmā* (self)", said the *Upaniṣadic* seers.

The transmission of lamp contains the rich treasures of Zen *Mondō*. One monk named *Chosui-Shisen* of *Śuṅga*-dynasty asked a question from Zen-master—Rōshi – named *Roya Ekaku*:

Monk :	"The originally pure—how can the mountains and the rivers and great earth come out of it?"
The Master :	"The originally pure—how can the mountains and the rivers and great earth come out of it?"

The master repeats the question itself, because this metaphysical problem is such that it cannot be answered in any logical form. The Zen-masters have made such metaphysical problems more enigmatic to make it clear to the disciple that such problems cannot be put into a linguistic form. The original pure is "*tathata*." It means reality which is devoid of all forms of particularization, it is neither existence nor non-existence nor both nor neither, because it transcends all categories of reasoning. All things in the world from beginning are neither matter nor mind nor consciousness nor non-being, nor being. The reality is inexplicable. However, it does not mean that there is no reality. It is the real itself which appears. The divine nature of reality is not unreal. The Zen-master would like to convey that the pure-being is beyond the reach of intellect. Hence, we cannot either affirm the existence of pure being or empirical world or we can deny the existence of pure being or empirical world. Those who maintain that the world exist are committing logical error because an examination we find that empirical world is essentially relative and hence unreal. Those who hold the view that it is non-existence are also committing the same mistake, because they are denying even the phenomenal reality to the empirical world. Our comprehension is essentially relative and hence we cannot comprehend the originally pure being because it transcends all the categories and reconcile all the antinomies of understanding. The Zen-masters would like to convey that exercising in metaphysic is utter fatality. The reality is beyond the grasp of intellect. It is non-dual reality in which all plurality is merged, it is to be directly realized. This is called Zen experience. This is called *Satori*.

Koan and Zen-masters

Who are the Zen-masters? This is a very searching question. According to the Zen traditional believe there have been 28 Zen patriarchs, the Śākyamuni is considered by the Zen school as its first patriarch followed by Mahākassyapa. According to Chinese tradition *Bodhidharma* is the first patriarch and Hui-Neng is the sixth and the last patriarch. Now, the question arises that why the other known great Zen-masters were not considered as the patriarch. What are the conditions and the qualifications traditionally laid down to confer someone the degree of patriarch? It is a very complex question. If we study the origin and the development of Zen Buddhism we cone to the conclusion that its development is based on Buddhist mysticism or esotericism. There is a definite impact of Buddhist tantrism on Zen thought and practice. Hence, it is but natural that Zen Buddhism has followed the Indian tradition of masters and disciple in transmission of the secret lesson on Buddhist *Yōga* and practice which is popularly known as *Dhyāna Yōga* from which the name of Zen Buddhism has originated. According to the ancient Indian mystical tradition the persons who have attained enlightenment fulfils the first condition to become teacher. However, there are other conditions and qualifications which one must acquire before he becomes a teacher. According to the *Tāntric* tradition to become a teacher one must have the spiritual power and capacity to perfect the *Bīja mantras*. The *mantras* are a mystical syllable incantation of which creates acoustic vibration which arouse the dormant divinity – the *Kuṇḍalinī śakti.* In *Mahāyāna* tradition the incantation of *mantras* and practice of meditation occupy important place. A teacher has the capacity to understand the spiritual weakness and the strength of disciple and after screening the mind and physiological structure of the disciple the teacher imparts necessary instructions to the disciple. This process is known as initiation – *Dīkṣā*. *Dīkṣā* or initiation is not what is taught in the modern universities by the teachers. It has the spiritual connotation and it is used in a very specific sense. This is probably the only valid method for the transmission of spiritual knowledge and technique which is followed almost in all the mystical traditions of the world religions. Zen Buddhism being an esoteric tradition it is no wonder that it is following the same *Guru-śiṣya paramparā*, teacher-student (disciple) tradition. Thus, the teacher what is called *Guru* in Sanskrit, or Indian tradition is very difficult qualification to attain for a lay man. All the enlightened beings cannot become a *Guru*. Strictly speaking there are only 28 Zen-masters and others have simply transmitted the line of thinking of this and that patriarch. The role of a Zen-master is most important in the life of every seeker of the truth and spiritual knowledge.

Like the ancient Indian *Guru* the Zen-masters have also follow the same technique of imparting spiritual instructions in the language which is known as *Sandhyā-bhāṣā* in India and *Koan* in China and Japan. This *Koan* is a spiritual lesson imparted by the teachers to the disciples. It stresses the mind of disciple which creates spiritual crisis and thereby the *Guru* paves the path for the ultimate liberation. The role of *Guru* becomes very important as he can alone save the disciples after imparting *Koan* lesson from becoming lunatic. It is moral and the spiritual responsibility of a teacher to gauge the capacity of disciple before imparting the *Koan* lesson. The teacher with his spiritual power which is known as sixth-sense he has capacity to have the direct vision and the knowledge of the truth and could judge the capacity of the disciple for the type and the intensity of meditational practice be imparted to a particular disciple.

From the very inception of Zen Buddhism it has emphasised the practice of meditation and *Koan* as the fundamental principles for the direct transmission of knowledge from teacher to disciple of the intuitive understanding and comprehension of reality (*tathatā*).

According to Zen tradition it was Śākyamuni Buddha who transmitted this sacred lesson and spiritual knowledge of understanding the reality, the *tathatā* to his disciple Kāśyapa and Kāśyapa in his turn transmitted this knowledge to Ānanda and in this way this transmission of knowledge and intuitive understanding of the reality continued for a long line of teachers and disciples until through Bodhidharma it was carried to China. Bodhidharma transmitted this secret lesson on *Dhyāna* to Hui-Ko known as Chinese Zen-masters. The Zen-masters have had a number of disciples to whom they transmitted this technique of *Bodhi-Jñāna.*

This transmission is called the *Śakti-patha*, in the Indian tradition. The teacher after screening the mental and the physical structure of the disciple, sometimes awakens the dormant divine power to make the disciple experience the spiritual knowledge and bliss attained daring the course of esoteric practice. Swāmi Rāmakrishna Paramahans awakened the spiritual power of Narendra Datta and made him realized the ultimate truth with this *Śakti-patha.* Swāmi Rāmakrishna Paramahansa succeeded in transforming the whole life of Narendra Datta and made him Vivekānanda. So, this tradition of transmission of knowledge and spiritual power is the quintessence of all the mystic-traditions. When disciple attains the same depth of intuitive understanding and spiritual power and realizes the same deepest truth then only the master put his final seal on the disciple's spiritual attainment, then only disciple attains the status of teacher and he may transmit the same knowledge to his disciple. At this state of spiritual sublimity both master and disciple see each other's inner eye to inner eye, which is called in Zen Buddhist phraseology "lock eyebrows together."

This tradition of transmission of knowledge and spiritual power continues in modern Japanese school of Zen Buddhism even today. In modern Japan only those person either priest or a layman who have received authentic transmission from an authentic teacher can alone impart the spiritual knowledge and training to others. Such teachers are conferred the title of *Rōshi* (the Zen-master). It is *Rōshi* or the authentic Zen-master who is entitled to guide his students to the Zen experience of awakening the inner-being by means of *Koans*. The monks or the priests or the layman who have studied and practice Zen, but have not received the transmission of spiritual knowledge and power from authentic teachers are not entitled to be called Zen-masters and as such they cannot impart training on Zen Buddhism. If such persons write and deliver lectures on Zen Buddhism and if people attain their lectures and read what they have written, they do so with the understanding that such persons are delivering lectures and writing from an incomplete understanding of Zen.

The Zen students during the Tang and early Śuṅga period recorded the profound religious understanding of the Zen-masters which are in form of *Koan*s. These *Koan*s form the basis of Zen doctrine and experience. To this collection of *Koan*s some of the *Mahāyāna Sūtras* and tile stories from the lives of the Zen-masters were added. Both Füller Sasaki says that, "these *Koan*s and the stories contain seed-words or the phrases, the master had uttered." The seed words is called *bīja-mantra* in *Tāntrika* tradition. It is of great esoteric significance. According to this esoteric tradition of both Hindu and Buddhist the incantation of *Bīja-mantra* form the essential path of meditation practice. The incantation of *Bīja-mantra* aims at awakening the dormant divine power and the inner being of man. The disciple when acquires merit after practicing for sometime the preliminary lessons becomes eligible for the initiation into *Bīja-mantra*. Same is the case with *Koan*s practice also. A seeker after truth approaches the Zen-master, in whom he has implicit faith for Zen lessons. The seeker humbly and respectfully approaches the Zen-master to accept him as a disciple. After getting the approval the student gets instructions in practice of *Zazen*. The student is taught a lesson on the *Zazen* practice. That is a lesson on the mode of sitting, breathing and concentration. After practicing *Zazen* for some time when the student becomes verse in *Zazen* practice he is being put to test whether he has acquired a good seat and has become proficient in concentration or not. When a student passes the test he acquires the merit to get initiation into *Koan* practice.

The Zen-master takes an interview which is known as *Sanzen,* which is conducted in a formal way. After ascertaining the merit on eligibility of the student the master imparts lesson on *Koan* which is to be meditated upon. And from there the relation of teacher and student becomes a very intimate. Student visits at an interval the masters to seek guidance end ascertain whether he is proceeding on a right line while meditating on *Koan* or not when student attains right insight into the *Koan* the master put to him further test in this way the practice of the *Koan* continues under the direct supervision of teacher until the disciple attains *Satori*.

The practice of the *Koan* is being done under the supervision of the *Rōshi* Zen-master to ensure that the student's mistaken notions and illusions are discarded one by one and he must attain the right understanding and perception of each *Koan*. The each *Koan* depicts some aspects of the truth and with the constant practice of the different *Koan* student is made to realize the ultimate reality which consists the total of Zen philosophy and doctrine. The doctrines of the Zen Buddhisn has not been enunciate in linguistic form because Zen is not a concept, but it is a direct experience of reality and this is why it is said that, Zen-master teaches his student "WU" that is nothing. The Zen-master teaches his student means that the knowledge does not come from outside. The master guides his disciples in such a way that he realizes the truth which lies in his own being. There is old Chinese saying "The treasure of the house do not come in through the gate." The truth lies deep within one's own being, it is to be awaken and revealed through our own spiritual practice.

The life of the Zen-master has confirmed that the *Zazen* is only method to which one can attain *nirvāṇa*. The Buddha was a born seer, but he practiced *Zazen* for six years until he attained supreme enlightenment. So was the case with Bodhidharma, the first Chinese patriarch. Bodhidharma practiced meditation for nine years facing the wall until he attained total liberation. Dōgen the founder of the *Sōtō* school says that, *Zazen* is the gateway to total liberation. And this is why the practice of *Zazen* and resolving of the *Koans* are the corner-stone of Zen Buddhism.

As we have already stated that the *Zazen* is the foundation of Zen, but we should bear in our mind that it is not just any kind of sitting in lotus-posture, back-strata, breathing properly, mind concentrated beyond thought, would awaken and bring enlightenment. Meditation is a very complex process. Meditation includes the incantation and the recapitulation of the reality (*tathatā*). In the words of Dōgen one must see with the sense of dignity and grandeur like a mountain or giant pine tree, and with a feeling of gratitude towards the Buddha and the patriarch, who made manifest *Dharma* and we must be grateful for our human body through which we have the opportunity to experience the reality of the *Dharma* in all its profundity. Thus, we find that the role of the master occupies eminent position in all the mystic traditions of the world without the help and guidance of a teacher one cannot get into Zen Buddhism.

Notes

1. *Tractatus*, 6.42.
2. *Sitaro se age jahan aur bhi hai. Abhi iske intahan aur bhi hai.*
3. *The Three Pillars of Zen*, p. 65.
4. *Essays in Zen Buddhism* (*Second Seires*), D.T. Suzuki, Buiddhist Society, London: Rider & Company, (1950), p. 87.
5. *The Three Pillars of Zen*, Philip Kapteau, Boston, U.S.A.: Beacon Press, (1965), p. 64.
6. *Tadā drastu svarūpe avasthānām, Patañjali Yoga Sūtra.*
7. *Ch'an and Zen teaching*: Lu K'uan Yu, the Clean Light Series, Berkely, Shambhala, U.S.A., (1970), p. 10.
8. *Zen: A Way of Life*, p. 112.
9. *Studies in Zen*, D.T. Suzuki, Published for the Buddhist Society, London, by Rider, London, Second Edition, (1957), p. 107.

CHAPTER 5
The Concept of *Satori* (Enlightenment)

Satori and Enlightenment

Satori is a state of Enlightenment. It is a spiritual experience. It comes after practicing Zen technique of *Koan* and meditation. It is a process of inner realization which transcends all forms of dualism. This state of Zen experience is a state of consciousness, and not an annihilation. Dr. D.T. Suzuki says that "the knowledge contains in *Satori* is concerned with something universal and at the same time with the individual aspect of existence."[1] Thus, *Satori* stands for complete understanding of *Buddha*-nature. It is a form of inner perception and revelation. This experience of *Satori* comes only after uprooting of all thoughts, all imageries, all memories. In short it comes with the uprooting of all forms of I-ness. This inner experience of the ultimate reality *tathatā* destroys all forms of self-identifications and attachments. The experience of *tathatā* takes place in the deepest level of consciousness.

The concept of *tathatā* forms the philosophical foundation of Zen Buddhism. The *Prajñāpāramitā Sūtra* forms the earliest basis of *Mahāyāna* school of Buddhism. The basic philosophical ideas and concept of this school have been expounded in this *Sūtra*. The Buddha has been referred as *tathāgata* (*tatha+agata* or *tathā+gata*), which means the one who has "thus gone" or "thus come", is an epithet of the Buddha used by him when speaking of himself.

Suchness is the essence of *tathāgata*, for without it Buddha is not *tathāgata*. It means he is not such as he is that is, he is know more 'I'. But this suchness does not belong to Buddha only, it is possessed by all beings. Suchness is the reality. Reality is that which neither come nor goes out; nor it is subject to destruction nor to obstruction nor to discrimination. According to *Mahāyāna* philosophy as long as we hold it within ourselves we partake in the suchness of *tathāgata*, because in our essential existence and reality we are neither born nor dead. In this ultimate sense *tathāgata* along with all beings are one. When we talk of all beings in ultimate sense we do not talk in the relative sense of matter or mind, because the truth is that, a thing or being is born or passes away in the suchness of *tathāgata*. Our discursive knowledge touches the phenomenal (*Samvṛti*) aspects of reality not the transcendental (*Paramātma*) aspects of reality. From the empirical point of view a man comes and goes away, but from the transcendental point of view the birth and death are an illusion. Truth is that a man is born and passes away in the suchness of the *tathāgata*. However, *Prajñāpāramitā-sūtra* warns against the misuse of suchness to be regarded as suchness. In that case it is not suchness. The suchness of *tathāgata* is suchness of all beings and hence suchness does not have say pluralistic character. The concept of suchness is not creation of any logical reasoning and hence, it cannot be comprehended by our senses and mind. The experience of this ultimate reality (*tathatā*) is *satori*, which is unthinkable, unrepresentable, unnamable and indescribable and it is because of the transcendental nature of *Satori* one who tries to understand it with the help of logical mind one enters into the world of contradictions, negations and antinomies.

After realizing the limitation of thought and language in communicating the Zen experience which is incommunicable, the Chinese Zen-masters developed a new concept of "Wu" to describe this state of consciousness which is beyond the realm of discrimination and differentiation. The literal meaning of this Chinese term "Wu" is nothingness or no mind. However, the experience of "Wu" has a some difference in quality and duration of the flash of intuitive awareness of *nirvāṇa*. The awareness of nothingness is not the end but the beginning of Zen meditation. After this "breakthrough" to the practice of no thought or no mind a man attains maturity in Zen meditation which enables him to have the direct and total experience of reality *tathatā* which is non-duality. This state of Zen experience cannot be communicated either with the help of language or symbolism or any other ways but it can be experienced through a long and continued practice of Zen meditation. The Zen meditation opens the inner eye of man which makes the unspoken doctrine realized as living truth.

In *Pāli-nikāyas* (*āgamas*—in Chinese) *nirvāṇa* is said to be state of complete extinction of greed (*lōbha*), hatred (*dōṣa*) delusion (*mōha*). This state of supreme end can be attained with our own effort. It cannot be attained either with the help of someone or with the blessings of God.[2]

Satori or *nirvāṇa* is a state of eternal bliss. In this state of eternal bliss one attains a state of complete purity, and one experiences highest and unchangeable happiness. *Nibbāṇa* is the highest bliss.[3] It is like crossing the other side of the river. The *suvarṇabrabjasa* (Chinese translation) enumerates many characteristics of *nirvāṇa.* Following are some of the characteristics of *nirvāṇa* as enumerated by *suvanna-brabjasa.* (1) All evil passions so arise from greed, but *tathāgata* is free from greed. The freedom from greed is called *nirvāṇa.* (2) If the *tathāgata* is free from greed he is not attached to anything and as he is not attached to anything he neither comes into being nor goes out of being and this is called *nirvāṇa.* (3) As he neither comes into being nor goes out being he is the *Dharmakāya* which abides for ever and this is called *nirvāṇa.* (4) What is beyond birth and death is beyond description. This is called *nirvāṇa.* (5) There is neither subject ego nor object world and all that see due to the constant changing of conditions, and what is unchangeable is called *nirvāṇa.* (6) All evil passions are errors do not defile the *Dhamma*-nature. *Dhamma*-nature remains as it is. It neither comes into being nor goes out of being. This is Buddhahood, and this is *nirvāṇa.* (7) Suchness alone is real and all the rest are conditional truth. Suchness is reality which is *tathāgata* and it is called *nirvāṇa.* (8) In reality there is nothing like falsehood or subject to argumentation. Reality is beyond the discursive knowledge and conditional understanding of truth. This truth is understood by the *tathāgata* and it is called *nirvāṇa.* (9) What is unborn is real and what is born is unreal. The ignorant souls are drowned in the ocean of birth and death, while *tathāgata* is beyond it, which is called *nirvāṇa.* Unreality rises from conditionality whereas reality transcends it. According to *Mahāyāna tathāgata Dhamma-kāya* is reality. It is called *nirvāṇa.*

The *Mahāyāna* Buddhism believes in *Trikāya, Nirmāṇa-kāya, Dhamma-kāya* and *Sambhōga-kāya. Nirmāṇa-kāya* is the physical body which is born, suffers decay and death. *Dhamma-kāya* is the essence of reality. It is neither born nor suffers decay and death. It is beyond all conditionality. It is *tathāgata* and it is reality. *Sambhōga-kāya* is the spiritual and eternal body of the Buddha who lives in the heavenly world known as *Tusita*. *Theravāda* tradition does not believe in *Trikāya-vāda*.

Nirvāṇa has been viewed as complete emptiness in *Mahāyāna* tradition. The total elimination of the feeling of I-ness results into complete emptiness. This state of perfect emptiness is a state of enlightenment. Lord Buddha defines the state of *Satori* as immortal element (*amaladhātu*); because it is the only element that does not suffer decay and death. It does not perish, because it is free from craving (*lōbha*), aversion (*dōṣa*), ignorant (*mōha*). When a man becomes free he attains freedom from the idea and feeling of I-ness. In this state of freedom there is no trace of craving and no chance of clinging to self-hood and thus, there is no question of decay and death. This state of freedom from craving put an end to decay and death and this is why it is called immortal element.

An enquiry into the nature of *nirvāṇa* or *Satori* raises another problem that is whether it is attainable in this very life or a person will have to wait till his death. In depth study of nature of *nirvāṇa* throws some light on this vexed problem. There are two kinds of *nirvāṇa* according to Buddhism: (1) *So-padisesa-Nibbāṇa-dhātu* and (2) *Anupadisesa-Nibbāṇa-dhātu*. *So-padises-Nibbāṇa* means that a person has attained enlightenment but he has to exert his predetermine-kārmic energy (*Saṁskāra*). Though the mind of the enlightened person becomes free from all sorts of defilements and delusion, but he has to bear the mental-body to exhaust the last trace of meta-psychosis. The unattached mind of the enlightened person has been compared with the water on the leaf of the lotus. Therefore, during the first state of *So-padisesa-Nibbāṇa*, a man attains intermittent release from suffering because, in spite of the attainment of enlightenment he still exists as an individualized person subject to the suffering of residual *kamma*. There are innumerable examples in Buddhist history. The Buddha himself injured by Devadatta, Venerable Mahāmoggallāna was beaten to death by criminals, and Venerable Aṅgulimāla was humiliated and beaten while he was walking with the begging bowl. These persons suffer humiliation, injury and death because of their residual past *kamma*.

Anupadisesa-Nibbāṇa means the final liberation from the cycle of birth and death. A man attains this state of *Nibbāṇa* after consuming of all the aggregates (*Saṁskāras*). There is no chance of rebirth anymore. A man takes birth to consume his kārmic energy acquired during his previous birth. A man is reborn to serve the chain of dependent origination at the link where feeling is followed by craving. Without practicing meditation and attaining *nirvāṇa* a man serves the endless cycle of birth and death where becoming leads to a new birth.

On the problem of what happens to the *Arhat* after death is one of the controversial philosophical issues which has generated enough argument for and against the existence of abiding reality. The *Theravādī* interprets in the light of principles of dependent origination and says that the enormous believe in an avoiding reality is the root of all confusion. Buddha has already stated that there is no ability entity. It is an illusion. Life is a process of becoming. Since, there is no personal self, there is no question of its existence after the death when the *Arhat* dies the psychomental process comes to an end for the lack of the fuel needed to keep it going on. The fuel is craving (*tanhā*) which leads to grasping and grasping in term leads to further becoming. If the craving is totally extinguished there can be no further becoming. When the body dies at the expiration of all the kārmic energy there is no possibility of further taking rebirth. If there is no rebirth there is no decay, disease and death. If there is no decay, disease and death there is no suffering, no lamentation or despair. This is the end of suffe·ing. This is a state of *Satori*.

The state of *satori* comes after the enlightenment. The enlightenment is a perception to see thing as it is and not thing as it appears. This dawn of the *Bodhī-Jñāna* simply changes the perspective of our life and this change of perspective liberates man from the trammel of neiscense. Like Vedānta, *Mahāyāna* believes in two kinds of realities, *Saṁvṛtti-Satya* and *Pāramārthika-satya*. So long a man lives in the world of subject and object of *Samvṛtti-satya* he does not have the perception and vision *Pāramārthika-satya* because of the fact that man is afflicted with ignorance. He does not have the power and the privilege to apprehend the ultimate reality directly. The meditation generates the meditative insight in man and enkindles his being and as a result he has the direct knowledge and vision of the ultimate reality (the Buddha-nature). This realization of Buddha-nature transforms the whole perspective of man. In Vedānta it has been illustrated through a beautiful metaphor of goldsmith's perception of gold. A layman sees the piece of gold in different forms and names, like rings, neckless etc., but when the same gold ornaments put before goldsmith he sees the real essence of the ornaments, that is gold. Likewise an enlightened person is one who sees the real essence of thing and being that is *tathatā*. This real mode of perception of essential nature of thing and being is enlightenment. The result of enlightenment is final release from the bondage of all kinds of suffering. This is called liberation. This is called *nirvāṇa*. Thus, the *Satori* or *Nibbāṇa* is the result of enlightenment.

Satori and Absolute Freedom

The *Satori* is a state of Absolute Freedom. In *saṁskṛta-nirvāṇa* is called *Mukti* in Pāli: *mutti*. However, this state of freedom is not a negative state. A negative word need not necessarily connotes a negative state. The Pāli or the Sanskrit words for health is *Ārogya*. This word *Ārogya* is a negative term which literally means absence of illness. But *Ārogya* does not mean a negative state. It has a positive impact. The word "immortal" in Sanskrit is called *Amṛta*, in Pāli *Amata*, is a negative term, but it does not denote negative state. However, *Satori* has a negative meaning also, because this state of freedom is a liberation from craving (*Lōbha*), ill will (*Dōṣa*) and ignorance (*Mōha*). This state of absolute freedom is liberation from dualism of subject and object, relativity of ti ne, space and causation and state of conditional reality. In absence of freedom from rational understanding of things and being man can never catch himself. He stumbles at this or that perceptions and feelings without the meditative insight end vision a man enters into the world of puzzlement. This is bondage. *Laṅkāvatāra-sūtra* says that, "Ignorant people get stuck in the world like elephant get stuck in the mud." *Laṅkāvatāra-sūtra* would emphasise on the right understanding (*Sammādiṭṭhi*) for the attainment of *Satori*. The whole Buddhist philosophy veers around the attainment of enlightenment or *Satori* as the supreme end of one's life. Its approach is both scientific and practical. To illustrate this point the Buddha has explained to Māluṅkya, that if a man had been pears by an arrow it would be seer foolishness on the part of victim to inquire from the doctors about his caste (*gōtra*), colour (*vaṇṇa*) and creed (*dharma*). The most scientific and the practical approach in such circumstances is to get the arrow out from the body to save the patient. Zen Buddhism following the teachings of Buddha put emphasis on the practice of meditation for the attainment of *satori* which is cessation of all kinds of sufferings and bondages. Philip Kapleau says: "The drive towards enlightenment is powered on the one hand by a painfully felt inner bondage – a frustration with life, a fear of death, or birth – and on the other by the conviction that through *Satori* one can gain liberation. But it is in *Zazan* that the body-mind's force and vigour are enlarged and mobilized for the breakthrough into this new world of freedom."[4]

This freedom and the experience of revelation brings about a metamorphosis in the life of Zen practitioner. It is a veritable psychological mutation of thought and vision. This state of experience of *satori* cannot be expressed and analysed by our available semantic of language. However, this state of *Satori* is being defined in the following terms:

1. *Supra-rationality*

The experience of absolute is not the result of any rational process. On the contrary the discursive knowledge and imagination and prefiguration create obstacles in realizing the Zen experience of *satori*. The discursive knowledge and conditional reality bind the man with the cycle of birth and death, sufferings and delusion. The authentic experience of *satori* is beyond the category of logic and reasons.

2. *Meditative Insight*

Authentic *satori* experience is beyond the reach of senses and the mind. There is an element of inner seeing and experiencing the essential nature of one's own being and existence which is called Buddha-nature. This state of freedom is not annihilation.

This state of Zen experience liberates man from the snares of false subjectivity which creates false distinction between *Saṁsāra* and *Nirvāṇa*. According to Zen Buddhism reality or *tathatā* is non-dual. It is the knowledge attained in *satori*, is concerned with the experience of the essential nature of things and beings which is called *Svāvakṣaṇa*. This knowledge is incommunicable and indescribable.

3. *Authentic Experience*

Satori is an authentic experience of ultimate reality. It is elimination of all thoughts and all memories born out of metapsychosis (*Saṁskāra*). It is an evident of one's inner perception which originates from the inner perception. It is free from all kinds of self-identifications and attachments.

4. Inner Awareness

Nirvāṇa is an inner awareness. It cannot be a (*bhāva* and *asaṁskṛta anupadāna*) at once. The experience of *satori* does not bring change in things and beings. There is a change in our way of perception. The function of meditative insight and experience is not to transform the real but only to create change in our way of perception. This change of perception or inner awareness is epistemic and not ontological. Reality is as it is. Zen Buddhism believes that there is no difference between neumena and phenomena (*Paramārtha* and *Saṁvṛtti*). They are neither separate entities nor two states of the same reality. *Tathatā* is the only reality. The *Saṁsāra* or the phenomena is created by false constructions when *tathatā* is seen through the thought forms of constructive imagination is the world of sense experience. When ultimate reality is experienced it is a state of freedom and *satori*. This is state of inner awareness which abandons the existential (*bhāva dṛṣṭi*) and not existential view points (*vibhāva dṛṣṭi*).

5. Indeterminate

Philosophically speaking *satori* is indeterminate and cannot be identified with consciousness or bliss. *Satori* is the transcendent life of the inner accesses. It is neither an ens (*bhāva*) or non-ens (*abhāva*) nor both nor neither.

6. Transcendental Wisdom

Nirvāṇa does not have any cosmological function. It is mystic experience which comprehends things and beings in their thusness. This concept of transcendental nature of *satori* flows from the *Mahāyāna* concept of *Prajñāpāramitā*. This concept of transcendental wisdom establishes organic relation with the original teachings of Śākyamuni. The theocratic philosophical teachings of Zen Buddhism is found in germinal form in teachings of Buddha. However, the fundamental concept of Buddhism undergone a significant change and transformation prompted by the religious requirements and aspirations of the people where it took root in the cultural malie of different lands. It is a significant philosophical development to notice that the different schools of Buddhism which emerged in course of time in different lands, claimed themselves as original teachings of the Buddha. The whole controversy veers round the concept of *nirvāṇa*. *Nirvāṇa* is the central concept of Buddhism.

Different concepts and interpretations are pointed to the transcendental nature of the wisdom attained in *satori*. It is indeterminate, ineffable and incommunicable experience which is known as *Prajñāparamita* transcendental wisdom. This intuitive cognition of *tathatā* which is invaded in things and beings is *satori* which comes after long and rigorous practice of meditation.

7. Spontaneity

The experience of *satori* is sudden and spontaneous. Dr. Suzuki says: "*Satori* comes upon us abruptly. It is an instantaneous experience." There is a controversy regarding the sudden and the gradual nature of *nirvāṇa*. This controversy has given rise to two schools of Zen Buddhism, namely *Rinzai* and *Sōtō* which we have already discussed in the previous chapter. However, we believe that *nirvāṇa* comes like a lightening. Suppose, there is a palace where no light has been lit for the last hundred years. If someone discovers that palace and lit the light it would brighten the whole palace with twinkling of an eye. In no case it would take hundred years to remove the darkness. Likewise, a man is under the influence of *lōbha*, *dōṣa* and *mōha* which causes bondage and this process continuous life after life until man attains enlightenment. With the attainment of enlightenment man attains absolute freedom suddenly and spontaneously.

The perfect instantaneity is a result of continual psychological disassociation from *Kāmatanhā*, craving for sensual, pleasure, *Bhāvatanhā*, craving for existence and, *Vibhāvatanhā* craving for non-existence. This inner awareness is attained by the practice of non-difference self and the external world, between mind and its contents. The experience of *satori* is a complete liberation from all mental habits and dispositions.

The *Udāna* makes in-depth study of nature of *nirvāṇa*. In the four discourses given below the *Udāna* analyses the concept of *nirvāṇa* (*Nibbāṇa paṭisaṁyutta*).

1. "There is, monks, that sphere wherein there is neither earth nor water nor fire nor air; there is neither the sphere of infinite space nor of infinite consciousness nor of nothingness nor of the sphere of neither perception nor non-perception; where there is neither this world nor the world beyond, nor both together, nor moon nor sun; this I say is free from coming and going, from duration and decay; there is

no beginning nor establishment, no result, no cause; this indeed is the end of suffering.

2. Non-substantiality is indeed difficult to see. Truth certainly is not easily perceived. Craving is mastered by him who knows, and for who sees, there is nothing.

3. Monks, there is a not-born, not-become, not-made, not-compounded. Monks, if that not-born, not-become, not-made, not-compounded, were not, no escape from the born, made compounded would be known here. But, monks, since there is a not-born, not-become, not made, not-compounded, therefore, an escape from the born, become made compounded is known.

4. For him, who is attached, there is vacillation; for him who is not attached, there is no vacillation.

> When there is no vacillation, there is calm;
> when there is calm; there is no delight;
> when there is no delight, there is no coming-and-going; when there is no coming-and-going, there is no disappearance-and-appearance; when there is no disappearance-and-appearance, there is nothing here nor there or between them; this indeed is the end of suffering.

The close examination and analysis of these spheres signified, that, *nirvāṇa* is absolute liberation from craving. A man who attains *nirvāṇa* remains unmoved and unattached. However, it does not mean that, the man who attains *nirvāṇa* does not experience pleasant or unpleasant, happiness or unhappiness. As a result of the cessation of cravings man does not suffer from worldly-worries like birth and death, decay and disease and coming or going.

Satori and Oneness

Like any other non-dualistic philosophy and religion, *Mahāyāna* tradition believes that one and the same reality is viewed as neumenan and phenomenon world. In common parlance, it is said that, the non-dual philosophy believes in two truths, the *Paramārtha-Satya* and the *Saṁvṛtti-Satya*. This conceptual distinction is implicit in almost all the absolutistic traditions. It is not that Nāgārjuna propounded the philosophy of *Paramartha-Satya* and *Saṁvṛtti-Satya* which constitute the reality that is *Śūnya*. Nāgārjuna made explicit which was implicit in the original teachings of the Buddha. The Buddha has also considered *nirvāṇa* as absolutely real and *Saṁsāra* as conventionally real.[5] This doctrine of two truths and non-dual was fully developed in the philosophy of Nāgārjuna and Buddhist *tantra*. According to Buddhist *tantra Prajñā* and *Upāya*, *Śūnyatā* and *Karuṇā* constitute the absolute reality and realization of which called *nirvāṇa*. In *Hindu tantra* also *Śiva* and *Śakti* constitute reality.[6] From the absolutistic point of view the realization of Oneness with reality is enlightenment. The Zen Buddhist being the development of *Mahāyāna* tradition it owes its origin and development to Buddhist *tantra* also. According to Buddhist esotericism realization comes after the rigours of meditation and not by proxy. The enlightenment is a non-dual intuition of the absolute oneness. The real is non-dual and free from all predications and relations, categories and concepts. It is indeterminate, transcends and quiescent. Nāgārjuna has very rightly termed the reality as *Śūnya*, because it is bereft of all predications and relations. However, it would be wrong to believe that the doctrine of two truths advocated by non-dual schools is really two. *Prajñā* and *Upāya*, *Śiva* and *Śakti* are not two separate entities. They are the two faces of the same coin. One cannot be separated from the other. So, both from philosophical and practical point of view *Paramārtha* and *Saṁvṛtti* or *Nirvāṇa* and *Saṁsāra* constitute one and the same reality. The reality is one because it along with itself or *Akṛtrima svabhāva*. The Zen Buddhism has rightly said that, the same truth when it is viewed from transcendental point it is *nirvāṇa*, when it is viewed from empirical point it is *Saṁsāra*. Thus, the realization of this oneness is *satori*. *Śūnyatā* and *Karuṇā* are the two functions of *Bodhi Chitta*. *Śūnyatā* is *Prajñā*. It is identical with the absolute. *Karuṇā* is the operative principle which gives concrete manifestation to *Śūnyatā* in phenomena. The one is transcendental and the other is imminent. However, this reality is beyond the reach of categories of reason and senses.

Now, the question arises how to experience the *satori* (enlightenment). This is a philosophical problem which needs careful examination and analysis. *Absolute* or *Śūnyatā* is absolute it does not need any proclamation to be declared so. If our knowledge is to constitute it the absolute will cease to be absolute. Truth is impersonal and transcendental. *Śūnyatā* or *Prajñā* is *Dharmatā* the intrinsic nature of all things and beings. And *tathatā* constitutes the eternal nature end essence of all. It is beyond the categories of existence and non-existence both or neither. A man is having a phenomenal existence how can claim to have knowledge of the absolute? All human experiences are in and through the categories of thought which are *Saṁvṛtti*. To solve this problem Buddhism introduced a concept of *tathāgata*, who is supposed to know the both aspects of the truth *Nirvāṇa* and *Saṁsāra*. Logical problem emerges by accepting *tathāgata* as an amphibious being mediating between *Paramārtha* and *Saṁvṛtta Satya*. It would be logically unsound to believe that a man lives in both the worlds one and the same time. A moment a man attains *nirvāṇa* he sheds his empirical existence logically he cannot say that he had attained *nirvāṇa*. Because He is not there to know that he has attained *nirvāṇa*. His whole being is transfigured with the attainment of *nirvāṇa*. There is no trace of HE is left anymore and this state of enlightenment is called in Zen Buddhism (no mind).

The WU-MEN-KUAN is one of famous treatises of Zen Buddhism. There are 48 cases which have been referred in this book. Hui-Kai (1183-1260) is the author of this book who flourished during the latter part of Śuṅga Dynasty in China. This Zen-master attained *satori* by the practice of the WU. In this book the first case that has been depicted by *Wu-Kuan* is that of a monk who approached Chao-Chou for Zen training. The monk asked, "Is the dog endowed with the Buddha-nature?" Chao-Chau replied: "WU." WU is a gateless gate that, leads to enlightenment. It is said that, when you practice, WU for long time your mind will gradually attain the state of oneness insight and outside. When, the practitioner attains this state of oneness he does not need to be told, because it is an experience which cannot be communicated. However, this state of oneness is neither state of emptiness nor a state of being and non-being. It is a meditational technique to emphasise the mind from its accumulated thoughts and meta-psychosis. Buddha himself has warned against the accumulation of all sorts of craving, which is the root cause of bondage. He has metaphorically explained that when you are crossing the sea of existence let not the water percolate in your life boat. If there is any water which has percolated you should throw away.[7] With the water of craving otherwise, O monk ! you would get lost in the sea of sufferings. Thus, the practice of WU is the practice of throwing the mental cravings out of mind and in this process of emptying the mind a state of no-mind (WU) is attained this state of no-mind is the state of supreme oneness. It is a state of mental equipoise and absolute calmness. D.T. Suzuki compares this oneness or the practice of WU with a dream of dumb person. A dumb person knows what he has seen in the dreams, but he is utterly helpless in communicating it to others.[8]

This state of mystic oneness is beyond the reach of categories of logic. The WU transcends both the limits affirmation and denial because of the limitation of thought and understanding intellect gets involved in antinomies when it attempts to comprehend the reality. The Zen-masters are conscious of the limitation of thought and reason in attaining *satori* and this is why they have taken the recourse of *Koan* practice through which one can attain the state of oneness unless you shun the reason, you cannot escape the contradiction. The Zen-masters are naturally anxious from the very beginning to ignore the seeing and to get whole of the unseen the WU. The WU is the bliss, the WU is liberation, the WU is oneness. The WU is *satori*. This unknown is the quest of Zen experience. However, the approach of Zen is not that of life of renunciation and self-denial. On the contrary, it is a life of fulfilment. The down-to-earth philosophical approach of Zen Buddhism gives complete satisfaction to our whole being. This whole being is non-being. And this non is transfigured into the no-mind. That is the WU.

All the mystic schools and traditions are unanimous that the spiritual experience of the enlightenment cannot be attained through the scriptural training. Zen Buddhism being one of the branch of mystic tradition it also believes that, the study of book cannot impart wisdom. It is necessary to acquire it from a master. However, one, cannot avoid the use of language. The Zen-masters devised a mystical language to convey the inner meaning and the message from master to disciple. This is known as *Koan*-practice. It is also a kind of language game in which, student is made to use his mind only to display the uselessness of mental faculties. The practice of *Koan* leads to the inner realization and the experience of the reality which pervades the whole universe. However, this reality cannot be explained by our day-to-day experience because it does not belong to the world of *Saṁvṛtti-Satya*. The practice of *Koan* leads to the oneness with the ultimate reality. This state of non-dual oneness is called *satori*.

Notes

1. *Essays in Zen Buddhism*, Vol. II, p. 29.
2. *Sudhi asudhi pacettaṁ naññо aññaṁ visodhaye* (*Dhammapāda*, V. 165)
3. *Nibbānaṁ paraṁ sukhaṁ, Ibid.*, V. 160.
4. *The Three Pillars of Zen*, p. 13.
5. *Majjhima-Nikāya*, N.II, p. 245 (Sutta, 140). *Etaṁ hi bhikkhus paramaṅ ariyasaccaṁ yad idam amosadhammaṁ nibbānaṁ.*
6. *Yoginī Hṛdaya*, p. 105, Vol. 7, Saraswati Granthmālā, Varanasi, Kaviraj, Dr. Gopinath (Ed.).
7. *Dhammapada, Yamakavagga*, 12 verse.
8. *Essays in Zen Buddhism*, p. 250.

CHAPTER 6
The Zen and Taoism

Zen and the Concept of Tao

Sixth century B.C. witnessed great birth of great philosophers. Whether it was an accident of history or grand design of the unknown, it is not possible to pass any definite judgement on the spiritual renaissance, moral awakening and intellectual ferment which took place in many parts of the world. Lao-tze and Confucius in China, Parmenides and Empedocles in Greece, Zarathustra in Iran and Mahāvīra and the Buddha in India were the founding fathers of the renaissance movement of the world. The import of their teachings are as fresh and lasting as they seem that there are the events of yesterday. Their teachings and philosophies had exercised great influence on the shaping of the civilizations and human destiny. Lao-tze, one of the greatest thinker of China was born in 604 B.C. in the village of Chu-Jhren. Lao-tze's real name was Li. He was addressed as Lao-tze as the mark of reverence to him. The word Lao-tze means Grand-master. It is said that when he was born his hair on his head was white. Almost all the historians and biographers agree that he was endowed with a great and original mind.

The teaching of Lao-tze is dry philosophical inquiry and metaphysical speculation. His book *Tao-te-kin* contains the lofty ideas and noble truth. *Tao* is the root concept of all Chinese thoughts. In common parlance it means the "WAY." The philosophical meaning of the word Tao is a code of conduct and the doctrine which unites man with the nature. Lao-tze has used this word in the sense of ineffable reality experienced in mystic ecstasy which lies at origin of the universe and within appearances. Thus, Tao stands for the absolute reality of other religions and mystical philosophy.[1] The concept of Tao and the concept of Buddha-mind or *Tathatā* have striking similarities. It is another fact of history that the Buddhism got ready acceptance by the Chinese mind when the Buddhist monk and scholars visited China in those ancient time which is known as ancient history, it was only because of the fact that Taoism and Confucianism had already prepared the moral and the intellectual ground for the easy germination of Buddhist thoughts. For the Chinese mind Buddhism was not an alien philosophy and religion like Christianity and Islam, but an extension of Taoism and Confucianism. Both Chinese intellectual and common man discovered in Buddhism the echo of their own philosophy and religion. Buddhism was transfigured and transformed into a new philosophy and religion which was the outcome of the confluence of three traditions—Buddhism, Taoism and Confucianism. As we shall discuss the impact of Confucianism on Zen Buddhism and Zen Buddhism's impact in Confucianism in another Chapter. Here we would like to confine our discussion on Taoist impact on Zen Buddhism and Zen Buddhism's impact on Taoism.

The concept of Tao has great similarity with the concept of reality according to Zen Buddhism. *Chung-tsu*, a philosopher of Taoism says: "The Tao cannot be affirmed to exist or not to exist, the name of Tao is merely an artifice for practical purpose, neither speech nor silence can convey it. Let us banish both speech and silence." In the same way Nāgārjuna says that reality is neither existence nor non-existence nor both nor neither. It comes to same as the banishing both speech and silence, when we would like to comprehend *tathatā* or the Tao. Both according to Zen Buddhism and Taoism the ultimate reality is beyond the reach of mind and senses. It is indescribable. However, it is the underlying essence and reality of all existence and being. Taoism calls it the principles of universal intelligibility and Zen Buddhism calls it Buddha-nature, which cannot be grasped, but can be revealed and experienced under the loving care of teacher.

The concept of *Mahāyāna* Buddhism that, the same reality when viewed from empirical point of view is *Saṁsāra* (world) and when viewed from transcendental point of view it is *nirvāṇa*. Thus, *Saṁsāra* and *Nirvāṇa*, constitute reality. They are like two faces of the same coin. This concept gave birth to a new doctrine of inborn *Buddha*-nature and it revolutionised the concept of salvation. Salvation was viewed as inborn nature of every man and woman. It is not to be assumed after ceaseless effort after many lives, but it is illuminating realization here and now of Buddha-nature which is ever present within. Swāmi Rāmakrishna Paramahansa has illustrated this point of view with a beautiful metaphor. Once a habitual pipe-smoker got out in the night and started in search of fire to lit his pipe with lantern in his hand. When he knocked the door of his friend and stated the purpose of his coming in the night, his friend said to him that why did he come to him in search of fire, pointing towards the lantern he said that he was already carrying fire with him. Likewise, salvation is the inborn reality, the very essence of ones being. It is a question of simply realizing this truth which is vailed by the ignorance and egoism. At this point the *Mahāyāna* Buddhism particularly Zen comes closer to the non-activity concept of Taoism. This cultural metamorphosis of *Mahāyāna* Buddhism with Taoism resulted into a new form of philosophical doctrine and religious practice known as Ch'an Buddhism (Zen Buddhism). Zen Buddhism imbibed the mystical philosophy of Taoism and enriched it with Buddhistic ideals and goals. Zen Buddhism is thus a cultural product of three philosophical schools, namely Buddhism, Taoism and Confucianism to meet the intellectual eye-earnings and the spiritual thirst of the Chinese mind.

Zen Buddhism greatly influenced the Confucianism also. The impact of the Zen Buddhism on the Taoism and Confucianism was so great and intense that it created tremendous intellectual stir and spiritual ferment, destroying some of the old and out modelled Confucian social norms heralded a new renaissance during the Śuṅga dynasty which was called learning of the Tao. This cultural movement created a new values and social reality. In this new movement Confucianism was transformed into Taoism and Taoism was transformed into Zen Buddhism. If we believe in the dialectical process of development, we can say, with certain reservations, of course, that if Confucianism was thesis Taoism was anti-thesis and Zen Buddhism was synthesis which retain the basic concepts of Confucianism and Taoism, but it blended them with higher concept of doctrine of no-mind—WU. This doctrine of no-mind has some similarity with Taoist concept of non-activity, but it is more sublime and lofty than Taoist concept of non-activity. The concept of no-mind of Zen Buddhism is a development of *Mādhyamikā* concept of *Śūnyatā* and *Tathatā*. However, there is a conceptual difference between *Śūnyatā* of *Mādhyamikā* and no-mind of Zen Buddhism. No-mind is not a concept it is an experience. Hence, it cannot be comprehended by the categories of reason, but through meditation.

The Buddhism was accepted as official religion of China because of its superior philosophy and religious practice. In the beginning Buddhism was denounced as barbarian religion. After going through the scriptural study and practicing Buddhism the same Chinese intellectuals who were at fixed in the beginning, started converting the moral and the social philosophy of Confucianism into a new religion, but due to the lack of religious appeal which binds man with infinite and man with society and ultimately man with himself to create harmony, peace, stability and progress, were abundantly lacking in Confucianism, and, hence, in spite of the best efforts of Chinese creative minds it would not be converted into religion. However, Taoism have had already assumed the status of a religion because of its profound mysticism, but it lacked the philosophical doctrine to provide infrastructure of a religious order.

These shortcomings of Confucianism and Taoism left with no alternative both for the Chinese intellectual and the masses, but to accept Buddhism and assimilate it into their own traditions. The Zen Buddhism is the result of this assimilation. Buddhism became very popular amongst the Chinese intellectuals because of its philosophical profundity and spiritual sublimity. The Chinese elites and educated started pleading for the acceptance of Buddhism as state religion. At the time of WU Dynasty the first emperor declared Buddhism as state religion, and this heralded a new spiritual awakening in China. The early Indian scholars who went to China to spread Buddhism were men of both intellectual achievements and spiritual attainments. Their spiritual wisdom and intellectual insight and logical mind and moral character kept the Chinese mind dazzled and captivated. This contributed much in the spread of Buddhism in China. The impact of Buddhism was great and lasting on Chinese life. It introduced new philosophical concepts such as concept of *Nirvāṇa*, Rebirth, Causality and *Karma* which were totally absent in Confucianism and Taoism. However, the concept of original Chinese way of liberation accepted readily the Buddhistic concept of *nirvāṇa*. The concept of liberation and way of the creative power of *Te Wen* considered as Taoist ideal. This Taoist concepts of liberation were assimilated in *Mahāyāna* Buddhism and they produced a new form of cultural life and philosophy known as Zen Buddhism.

There is another point of great similarity between Taoism and Zen Buddhism is that both the systems believe that centre of the mind's activity does not lie either in the conscious thinking process or in the ego. From the simple fact of nature Loe-tze drew the conclusion that, behind the manifold phenomenal existence of nature there exist a non-menonal reality. This reality is incomprehensible, but it manifests itself in laws of unfailing regularity. He calls this essential principle as Tao. Chung-tze (4th century B.C.) and Hanfei-tze (3rd century B.C.) have written commentaries on the teachings of Lao-tze. Chung-tze says "Tao is without beginning and without end." Further, he says that, Tao imparts form to form, but it is itself formless and as such Tao cannot have a name. Tao is source from which all things come into existence and to which all the things returned, through Taoists the means whom these takes place. It is like the *Brahman* of the *Upaniṣad*. It is eternal absolutely free. It is eternally at rest, but never ideal. It is omnipresent, immutable and self-determined, but at the same time it loves all things and does not act as ruler. Tao creates, preserves, nourished and protects all things. The concept of Tao has similarity with Buddhist concept of *Śūnyatā* which is also immutable and transcendental reality.

Teh is the realization of Tao. Tao-tze defines the *Teh* as self-realization or that which we can do in this present moment to be manifestation of Tao. *Teh* has the similarity with *karuṇā*. Thus, *Tao* and *Teh* constitute the absolute of Taoism. The *Śūnyatā* and *karuṇā*, *prajñā* and *upāya*, constitute the ultimate reality of *Mahāyāna* Buddhism. Taoism is an esoteric, mystic and pantheistic religion. Like Buddhism in some sense, Taoism also prescribes spiritual discipline for the attainment of immortality. There is a great resemblance between Buddhist enlightenment and Taoist immortality. This striking similarities and philosophical proximity between Taoism and *Mahāyāna* Buddhism initiated the process of cultural metamorphosis which gave birth to a new philosophy and religion known as Zen Buddhism.

Zen and the *Shintoism*

There is a believe that God has founded the Japanese nation who descended from heaven and established his state when the heaven and earth became separated. This primitive conception of deity of Japan is known as *Shintō* or *Kami-no-michi*, which means the way of God. Thus, *Shintōism* assumed the form of national religion of Japan. The literal meaning of the *Shintō* is "the way of *Kāmi*", i.e. the way of divine or *divine-path*. *Kāmi* means mystical superior divine. It symbolizes sacred or divine power. On analysis and critical examination of content and form of *Shintōism* we come to the conclusion that *Shintōism* is not a religious order having deep philosophical foundation. It is a complicated rituals and complex ancient believes the observations which have remained comparatively unchanged in spite of the revival movement which was led by theologians like Mabuchi (1697-1789 A.D.), Motoori (1730-1801 A.D.) and Hirata (1776-1843 A.D.). The deity of *Shintōism* is called *Kāmi*. The term *Kāmi* means high, swift, good, but it does not mean infinite, omnipotent, and omniscience being, which is conceived as essential attributes of almost all theistic religions. Mottori, the great *Shintō* theologian, described *Kāmi* as various deities of heaven and earth as well as the spirit which resides in Shrines. Even birds, beats, plants, trees, seas and mountains and all other which are dreaded and revered for the extraordinary and pre-eminent powers are also called *Kāmi*. All those things and beings which are AWE insprings are considered *Kāmi*. The great theistic existentialists Otto considered AWE as the essential characteristic of religion. *Shintōism* has even deified Japanese emperor successively as Mikados. Purity occupies prominent position in *Shintōism*. *Shintō* shrines are famous for their simplicity. The purpose of offerings is to propitiate Gods or to expiate offenses against them. The offerings are of cakes, fruits, vegetables, flesh of deer, pigs, hare and goats. From the examination of the *Shintō* rituals and offerings it is evident that *Shintōism* is still in its primitive form of religious order. In spite of the technological and scientific development of Japan national religion that is *Shintōism* still retains animistic and polytheistic elements. Thus, Japan presents a paradox. It is interesting from the sociological point of view to study how view of animism and polytheism have survived in modern Japan.

Japanese name for *mana*, invisible power, for spirits or Gods is *Kāmi*.[2] *Shintōism* also believes like Buddhist esoteric in the existence of male and female principles they are *Izanagi* and *Izanami*. According to the Japanese mythology when *Izanagi* returned from the underworld and vast himself from the water of his left eye emanated *Amaterasu* – the Sun-goddess. From the water of his right eye emanated *Tsuki-Yonei*, the Moon-god, and from the washing of his nose emanated *Susanowo*. *Susanowo* is considered the god of sea and storm and who is the ruler of dead. The Japanese regards themselves as descendants of *Amaterasu* and *Susanowo* and other procreating deities. The Japanese people consider themselves as a great national family who have divine origination.

Shintōism was greatly influenced by Confucianism, Taoism and Buddhism. Confucianism was first to reach Japan in fifth century A.D. and by seventh century A.D. it took firmer root in the cultural milieu. Under the influence of Confucianism particularly the concept of centralization of political power was developed into a national cult. The myths of various clans were combined and reorganized into Japanese mythology with emperor occupying as a nuclear centre. The *Kāmi* of imperial house and tutelary *Kāmi* of powerful clans symbolize the *Kāmi* of the Japanese nation.

The spiritual humanism, sublime philosophy and naturalistic ethics of Buddhism were assimilated and got easy acceptance by Japanese innovative minds. Buddhism was assimilated in the main currents of their cultural life. Buddhism became almost a state religion of Japan. Buddhism reached Japan in 538 A.D. and in eighth century A.D. it was accepted as religion of both the elite and the masses. Buddhism and *Shintōism* became the inseparable part of Japanese religious life. The Japanese scholars started interpreting *Shintōism* from Buddhist point of view and Buddhism from *Shintō* point of view as a result of this cultural metamorphosis the shrines of *Kāmi* got place in the principles of Buddhist Temples. *Devas* of Buddhism were regarded as the *Kāmi* of *Shintōism*. A new religious awareness was emerged out of this cultural metamorphosis and as a result of which Japanese people started believing that *Kāmi* like other creatives were said to be suffering, because they were unable to escape the endless cycle of birth and death. Buddhism provided religio-spiritual discipline to ameliorate the sufferings and get them liberated from the cycle of endless transmigration. Thus, from the mid-eighth century Buddhist temples were built within the precincts of *Shintō* shrines and the *Kāmi* priest started reading Buddhist *Sūtras* before *Shintō* deities (*Kāmi*). In the last part of the eighth century *Kāmi* were regarded as *Avatāras* or incarnation of Buddhas and *Bodhisattvas*. *Bodhisattvas'* names were assigned to *Kāmi* and Buddhist statues were placed even in the inner shrines of *Shintō* temples. In some cases even Buddhist priests were made incharge of *Shintō* shrines. According to *Encyclopaedia of Britannica*: "After 1192 during the *Kāmakūra*, theories of *Shintō* Buddhist amalgamation were established. Two representative examples of such amalgamation were *Shintō*gon-*Shintō* and *Tendai-Shintō*. According to *Shingon-Shintō* also known as Ryobu ("Two aspects") *Shintō* the principle source of whole universe was considered to be the cosmic Buddha. Mahāvairōcana also called Iehi-Jitsu ("One Reality"). *Shintō* only the Buddha-nature was the source of all things. These two sects also brought various Buddhist rituals of all esoteric nature into *Shintō*. Buddhistic *Shintō* was popular for several centuries and influence the majority of *Shintō* shrines until its extinction at the Meiji Restoration."[3]

Shintōism has a greater similarity with Hinduism. Like Hinduism *Shintōism* also believes in the essential divine nature of man. According to Upaniṣadic teachings (*Mahāvākyas*) such as *Tattvam asi* and *So'-ham*; *Shintōism* also believe that man being *Kāmi's* child his nature is essentially sacred and divine. Both according to Hinduism and *Shintōism* religious practices are directed against the removal of dust and impurities of thoughts and deeds. There is a pantheon of Gods and Goddesses both in Hinduism and *Shintōism*. The different Gods and Goddesses are the different expressions and manifestation of spiritual and divine yearning of man.

Shintōism believes that man is *Kāmi*'s child. This means that man has been given his life by *Kāmi* and as such his nature is sacred. Further, it means that life and personality of man are worthy of respect and hence man should respect the basic human rights regardless of race, sects and nationalities. There is a total absence of concept of original sin of semitic religions. On the contrary man is considered to have a primarily divine nature. Purification is considered as religious practice to remove the dust of craving and impurities that covers man's divine nature. This divine concept of man has great similarity with the concept of Buddha-nature, possessed by every man and woman. However, *Shintōism* does not have the ethical and the spiritual discipline to remove the impurities of the soul for the attainment of the enlightenment. Buddhist method of meditation provided spiritual anchor for every man. There were other factors for the spread of Buddhism in Japan. The Buddhist Gods were considered more human than the vague and the animistic gods of *Shintō*. The concept of *karuṇā,* which symbolizes by *Amita Buddha* captivated the Japanese minds. The profound and voluminous scriptures and the great intellectual as well as the spiritual attainments of Buddhist scholars and monks contributed much in popularising and propagating Buddhism in Japanese soil. The conception of future life which is totally absent in *Shintōism* caught the imagination of Japanese people. The eleventh and the twelfth century is regarded as the age of emergence of different Buddhist sects and schools in Japan. According to some historians this was age of decadence for Buddhism also in Japan due to the divergent philosophies and religious practices and as a result Buddhism lost its prestige and old glory. But the philosophical profundity and meditative practices of Buddhism got expression in the emergence of new Buddhist-sects known as Zen Buddhism. The Zen Buddhism advocated that neither scriptural learning nor renunciation from the world was necessary, but the one and the only method to attain salvation was to discover the essential Buddha in man's own being through meditation. Zen Buddhism exercised a great and wide appeal in China and Japan.

The Concept of Zen and Love of Nature

It goes without saying that Zen Buddhism has exercised great influence on the artistic. intellectual, social, moral and spiritual life of China and Japan. It nas moulded to some extent the Japanese character. The impact of this school upon Japan has been so great and pervading that it has supplied the *elan-vita* for her cultural life. Zen Buddhism became the social reality and spiritual experience because it goes deeper into source of cultural life. The Zen terms and symbols are not conceptual, but real direct and vital because the Buddha-mind or suchness is accepted as a concrete living facts of universe and not a philosophical abstractions of speculative mind.

Zen Buddhism is rooted in the facts and experience. It lives in the midst of reality. It does not believe in renunciation and keeping oneself away from world of names and forms. Zen is a mystic tradition. Its mysticism has an organic relation with nature. It pays total respect and love to nature. By loving nature it means that nature is not an object to be plundered and conquered but it is a friend, a fellow being who has life and consciousness and as such destined to attain Buddhahood. D.T. Suzuki says: "Zen purposes to respect Nature, to have Nature, to live its own life; Zen recognises that our Nature is one with objective Nature, not in the mathematical sense, but in the sense that Nature lives in us and we in Nature. For this reason, Zen asceticism advocates simplicity, frugality, straightforwardness, virility, making no attempt, to utilize Nature for selfish purposes." [4]

According to Zen Buddhism reality is one and indivisible. The non-dual concept of reality makes nature organically related with consciousness. *Śūnyatā* and *karuṇā* constitute *Bodhi-citta*. The concept of *karuṇā* invokes the sense of friendliness with all inanimate and animate beings. Buddhism does not conceive nature as an opposite power. Nature is not hostile to man, because it is manifestation of the same *Bodhi-citta* of which man is a conscious expression. The Buddha's life himself epitomises the love of nature. It was not an accident of history but a grand design of *Bodhi-citta* that the Buddha was born under a *Śāla*-tree at Lumbini, attained his supreme enlightenment under the *Bodhi*-tree at Bodhgayā, and passed away again under a tree at Kusinagar. The Buddha's love of nature has greatly influenced his teachings and religious-order. It was again not by sheer accident that Buddha was born on full-moon day, attained Buddhahood on full-moon day, and he passed away into *Mahāparinirvāṇa* on full-moon day of the same month of *Vaiśākha*. The Buddhist love of nature springs from the concept of eternal tranquillity. Zen Buddhism believes that aesthetic aspect of culture is closely related with the concept of reality and asceticism. Zen does not believe in abstractions and conceptualization of thought and reasoning because it is rooted in nature and concrete experience of life. The whole Zen literature is collection of *mondōs* and *koans* which are pregnant with deep philosophy of day-to-day life and experience. The Zen epistemology does not believe in concepts and precepts. If one wants to understand Zen one can understand it right away without philosophical deliberation. This doctrine of immediate, direct and integral grasping of reality is characteristic of Zen Buddhism. The Greek educated us on art of reason, Christianity on art of believe, Islam on art of brotherhood, Hinduism on art of spirituality and Zen Buddhism taught us art of meditation. It was in tune with the non-dualistic philosophy of Hindu mysticism. Zen Buddhism imbibes the main tenets of *Upaniṣadic* mysticism that reality is beyond the reach of logic and mind and it enriched it with *koans*, *mondōs* and *wu* no-mind. The concept of no-mind or no-activity of Zen Buddhism unites man with nature. Zen gives us a comprehensive outlook of the universe because it has a most penetrating insight into reality. It considers that whole world is pulsating because it springs from the depth of all existence. The pulsating nature of reality when realized transfers the perception and personality of a man. It has happened with Masanobu Fukuoka author of "*The One-Straw Revolution: An Introduction to Natural Farming*."

The case history of Fukuoka is that he was plant pathologist and was working with Yokohoma custom bureau. On one day morning at the age of 25 he had a strange experience which transfigured his whole life and made him Zen practitioner. He realized that man knows nothing and there is no intrinsic value and he felt that every action is futile and every effort is meaningless. He had a new experience and perception he became a successful farmer and a social philosopher. The whole basis of his philosophy is that nature is wiser than man. He realized that the best method of working is when it is performed without interfering from discriminating mind. With this realization he introduced a new concept of "do-nothing farming." He means there by for the natural farming and getting the optimum product. One should follow the philosophy of no-cultivation, no-ploughing, no-fertilizer, no-compost, no-weeding, either by tillage or herbicides.

It is but natural that this would shake even the traditional farmer who rejects modern chemical farming, but for Fukuoka it is an article of faith. No cultivation is basic to natural farming. According to him the earth cultivates itself naturally by means of penetration of plant roots and activity of micro-organism, small animals and earth-worms. He himself has not cultivated his field for over two decades, but he has received a very high harvest and it has also improved the fertility of the soil.

Fukuoka's experiment is successful because of his faith that nature is pulsative, it is a living organism, it is a biosphere and ecosystem. The different parts of nature by the interpreting and supporting they maintain a balance of nature. According to this Zen attitude even a blade of grass and earthworm have the utility to maintain a balance in ecosystem.

The Zen loves of nature is not a hallow philosophy, but it is an article of faith. The concept of the natural farming is based on the Zen Buddhism's concept that form is emptiness and emptiness is form. This speaks about the non-discriminating knowledge. This non-discriminating knowledge is the basis of do-nothing farming. In Zen Buddhism it is also called *Mahāyāna* Natural farming or non-active farming. Non-active farming does not mean to remain idle and the passive spectator. It means that to understand the basic philosophy and approach to reality. One should enquire from oneself what is the meaning of doing this and that, what about not doing this and what about not doing that? The answer to these problems would dispense us with many of the esteemed traditional practices of farming.

Fukuoka's experiment has revealed some new truth. He has neither ploughed nor weeded nor fertilized for last twenty-five years. But his harvest of rice per acre is the highest in Japan. This positive aspect of his philosophy and new reality has captivated the attention of pragmatic minds even though they might have been sceptical about his philosophy. Fukuoka has formulated four principles of his do-nothing farming, which is based on his empirical study and experience. He summarises his philosophy in the following way:

1. No cultivation or ploughing or turning of the soil.
2. Do not use fertilizer or prepared compost.
3. Do not weed out either by tillage or herbicides.
4. Do not depend on chemical for pest control.

Apparently the above principles and philosophy of do-nothing farming seems rude and shocking. Even to the traditional farmers who reject modern chemical farming or for example the concept of non-ploughing goes against traditional high yielding practices. But for do-nothing farming non-cultivation is fundamental basis of natural farming. According to the concept and believe of this system nature cultivates itself. It is in striking contrast with the another mode of farming. This goes against all the prevalent practices and believe.

The philosophy of natural farming makes sense only if nature is conceived as living organism. According to this philosophy right from the mammals to the insignificant insects have the utility and identity in maintaining the fertility and in balancing the biological community which is necessary both for the survival of the man and nature itself.

The natural farming is closely related with natural diet and natural living. Natural diet means maintaining the rhythm and the balance of nature. Seasonal food raised locally from traditional seeds is nutrition. This new concept of natural diet has proved the fertility of science of deities developed recently in the West, which is based on the caloric needs of human body. Such facts besides being insipid and low in vitamins and minerals lack certain spiritual and psyche elements. The natural diet makes differences between materialistic and scientific eating from non-discriminating diet of the natural man. This natural dieting is based on the concept of natural man which has emerged from the Zen Philosophy of no mind, non-activity. According to this system food has no readymade definition, rules or proportions, but it has emerged out of own natural requirement according to the local environment and the various needs of the person.

This concept of love of nature throw further light and promise in getting high yielding seeds. According to this system the sources of energy are unlimited. It is question of having right understanding and perception of nature. The so-called scientific method and technology in getting high yielding varieties of seeds runs counter to the natural productivity. The so-called scientific technology which is replacing the rich varieties which are timely tested and adopted to different climate, soil conditions and physical needs may prove dangerous trap for the whole future farming system. This development will also place the genetic control of whole community in a few hands. The scientific technique of chemical fertilizer and pesticide can cause irreparable damage to the soil and eco-system. The concept of love of nature and natural farming warns against the formulations of policy by academicians, economists and agro-experts whose thoughts patterns are based on the latest so-called scientific experiments carried out in Western universities. Behind adaptations and formulations of the policy is the accepted mental framework. That work of science is progressive and always right. This so-called scientific temper of the modern age which conceives all and nature quantitatively and naturalistically as objects of manipulation and social engineering, to break away from this harmful and unnatural approach to life and social reality requires a new philosophy and vision. Zen Buddhism provides the philosophical and empirical basis for survival of humanity through love of nature and down to earth philosophical approach to reality. It provides a new perception and technique for the betterment of human society and the new methods for human engineering. For the environmentalists, futurists and social thinkers and human engineers who seek a system of better humanity and better world may get some philosophical basis and technique from the Zen system of natural farming, natural dieting which provides way of living close to nature, and avoids industrial money making enterprise and scientism which is eating away the very vitality of natural and human existence. By exposing them to the danger of modern scientific development and technological advancement which is leading human world to the holocaust of nuclear war.

The Zen insight and philosophy go deeper into the very source of life and existence. Zen is truly religious because it is in close touch with reality. Zen lives and feels reality as we feel the sensation of our pulses. If we study Christianity and other religions we find that their approach to reality or God is conceptual and devotional whereas Zen Buddhism's approach to reality is very intimate and integral. The concept of suchness, emptiness (*Śūnyatā*) or *Bodhi-citta* is not philosophical speaking a concept it is an experience which binds man with nature. From this concrete experience originates the philosophy of love of nature. The love of nature is a concrete living facts of life not a philosophical abstraction of some speculative mind.

Zen is very much rooted in the world of facts and reality. It always lives in the midst of reality. It does not propagate the philosophy of keeping oneself away from worlds of names and forms. For Zen makes a humble blade of grass act as a Buddha-body sixteen feet high and, conversely, the Buddha-body sixteen feet high is as a humble blade of grass, Zen holds the whole universe, as it were, in its palm. This is the religion of Zen.

Zen is often thought to be a form of pantheism. Apparently, it is not and Buddhists themselves sometimes ignorantly subscribe to this view. But if it is taken as truly characterising the essence of Zen, it altogether misses the point; for Zen is most decidedly not pantheistic in the same measure as Christianity is. Read this dialogue between *Ummon* (Yun-men) and his disciple.

Monk : "What is the Pure Body of the *Dharma*?"
Master : "The hedgerow".
Monk : "What is the behaviour of the one who thus understand?"
Master : "He is a golden-haired lion."

When God is the hedgerow dividing the monastery grounds from the neighbouring forms, there is perhaps a faint suggestion of pantheism, we may say. But what about the golden-haired lion? The animal is not a manifestation of anything else, he is supreme, he is autonomous, he is king of the beasts, he is complete as he is. No idea is suggested here of the manifestation of anything in any form.

"The golden-haired lion", as it stands in Ummons statement, may not be quite intelligible, even with this short explanatory comment, to those who are not used to the Zen way of expression. To help them I may quote another Zen *mondō*.

Monk : I understand that, when a lion seizes upon in opponents whether it is a hare or an elephant be makes on tremendous use of his power-pray tell me what this power is.

Master : The spirit of sincerity (literally) the power of not deceiving him.[5]

According to *Rinzai* School when person lives with sincerity, he is said to be a golden haired-lion. He becomes an embodiment of sincerity, virility and divinity. In this process of authentic existence man is not a manifestation of reality or divinity but reality itself because he becomes the whole truth, the essence of all existence and being, i.e. *tathatā*. This way of understanding life and nature demonstrate the Zen love of nature. Some thinkers pronounced Zen as polytheism, but according to D.T. Suzuki this many is to be taken as corresponding to the sense of Gaṅgā.[6] Polytheism of Zen does not represent few thousands of gods but hundreds of thousands of *kotyi* of Gods. It means each individual is an epitome of reality. Each individual is *Bodhi-citta*. It means each individual is related intimately and organically to all other individuals. This infinite organic an interrelationship is based on the philosophy of *Śūnyatā*. This Zen Buddhistic concept of reality constitutes the central core of love of nature. Love of nature is not to be understood in its literal common sense, but it is rather to be lived and felt the pulsating vibration of the universal principle of existence and being that is *Bodhi-citta* (Buddha-mind)."

The Zen conception of aesthetic is based on Zen mysticism. In both there is an absence of selfhood. The dualism of subject and object does not exist in Zen aesthetic end mysticism as they are merged in one absolute *Śūnyatā*. Zen Buddhism explains this basic fact of experience in and through anecdote and question and answer sessions known as *innen* and *mondō* respectively. Those who are not been initiated into Zen mysticism these *innen* and *mondō* are non-sensical statements. We cite the following *mondō* to explain the inner meaning of Zen aestheticism. Rikko, a government official of Tang dynasty talk to Zen-master Nansen.

Heaven and earth and I are of the same root. The tenth thousand things and I are of one substance. Is it not this most remarkable statement? The Zen-master Nensen drawing his attention of Rikko towards the flowering plant in the garden said, that the people of the world look at these flowers as they were in the dream. This *mondō* explains the aesthetic aspects of Zen Buddhism. It is truism that most of us do not really know how to look at the flower and appreciate the beauty of the nature. One can have the perception and experience of the beauty of nature only if one can have the experience of heaven and earth and oneself belonging to the same root. This experience of reality alone provides the philosophical basis for the experience of natural beauty and the aesthetic sense. The Japanese love of nature is intimately related to Zen because the experience of natural beauty springs from natural living.

According to Zen Buddhism mere experience of oneness is not enough for having the aesthetic experience of nature. This experience of oneness no-doubt purifies our mind and consciousness, but for the aesthetic experience multiplicity is warranted. The people according to Zen Buddhism are not experiencing the beauty and the sublimity because of the lack of experience of unity in multiplicity. The beauty of nature can be properly appreciated and experienced only when one could referred it to the universal and the essential being of all existence. This experience of unity in multiplicity does not come through philosophical disputations and argumentations. Zen-masters Nansen says, that experience of the beauty of nature can be experienced when a flower is reflected in own's mirror of consciousness. Thus, the aesthetic experience according to Zen is a religious experience.

To illustrate the aesthetic of Japanese culture we would like to cite a Zen poet who was a founder of Zen monastery in the province of Omi. His name is Jakushitsu (1290-1367):

> "The mind stirs the flying waterfall and sends in
> refreshing music;
> The moon is risen over the opposite peak and
> the bamboo shadows are cast over my paper window:
> As I grow older, the mountain retreat appeals
> all the more strongly to my feeling;
> Even when I am buried, after death, underneath the rock,
> my bones will be as thoroughly transparent as ever."

This poem gives a beautiful description of the natural beauty. But one cannot catch the central idea of this poem unless one can understand transparency of nature. In the absence of transparency it is but natural that after reading the above poem one would think that the poem gives a feeling of solitude and quietness. But according to Jakushitsu a poet is not a poet unless he is saturated with the feeling and the experience of reality. It is rightly said that the Zen Buddhism has provided a philosophical and religious basis to the Japanese love of nature. Sir George Sanson has rightly observed that, "the Japanese aristocrats, monks and artists who were moved by believe that all nature is permeated by one spirit. It was the aim of Zen practitioner in particular perjuring his mind of egotistic commotion to reach a tranquil intuitive realization of his identity with the universe."[7]

The concept of spiritual identity through which one can maintain eternal tranquillity by perjuring once egotistic commotion is an enchanting thought. This is a western way of solving the Eastern mysticism. However, the Zen intuition is somewhat different from the Western way of explaining Zen mysticism. The Western minds are ridden with concepts. They do not live in facts to explain the above conceptual difference between the Western way of explaining the Zen intuition and the Zen way of experiencing reality. We would like to quote the following *mondō*:

> "Chosha, of the T'ang dynasty, one day came back from a walk in the mountain. When he reached the monastery gate, the head monk asked, where have you been all these times, Reverend Sir."
> "I am just back from my mountain walk"—replied the master.
> "I first went out in the field scented with grasses and then walked home watching the flowers fall."
> "Is there any expression here suggestive of tranquillity that is behind and through change?" or of identity that is perceptible between Chosha and the grasses and flowers among which he walked up and down?
> Chosha one evening was enjoying the moonlight with his friend Kyozan. Kyozan pointing at the moon, said, "Each person without exception has this, only that he fails to use it." Is this a suggestion of "one spirit", or "tranquillity"?
> Chosha said, "Just as you say; and may I ask you to use it?"
> As long as "identity" or "tranquillity" blinds your eyesight, how can you "use" it?

Kyozan: "Let me see how you see it." Did he then enter into *Nirvāṇa* eternally serene?

Chosha then kicked his brother-monk down to the ground. Kyozan, quietly rising, remarked, "O brother-monk, you are indeed like a tiger." (When this tiger, like the golden-haired lion, roars, one ghostly "spirit" so valued by the critics vanished and "tranquillity" is no more").

From the above anecdote it is clear that Zen attitude towards the nature is not that of identity or tranquillity. According to Zen nature is always in a state of flux and movement to stop its pulsation and to seek tranquillity is to kill the nature. Zen way of appreciating and loving nature is to destroy all the artificial barriers between man and nature. The transparency means to wipe the surface of mind's mirror, so that one can have the experience of beauty, reflected in one's own consciousness. There is innate aesthetic sense for beauty in Japanese people. However, Zen Buddhism provided philosophical and religious basis for their innate feeling for nature and Japanese love of natural attraction towards things which are beautiful. Japanese mind cultivated by Zen teachings nourished and refined their aesthetic sensibility. This refinement excited the moral discipline and spiritual intuition. To make it more clear we would like to quote few lines from Ryokwan, Zen monk belonging to the *Sōtō* school. His hut was built in the Northern part of the country facing the sea; from worldly point of view Ryokwan was a big fool. But he was very much loved and respected by the neighbours. He was a good poet. His solitary retreat on a mountain away from the modern crowd was broken into by burglar. Burglar did not find anything to take away. He was greatly disappointed. Realizing the disappointment and anguish of burglar Ryokwan was very much touched. The burglar left him with the outside made open from which a bright moon poured its soothing light into Ryokwan room. The poet in him was awakened and he wrote:

"A burglar failing to carry off the moon,
It shines in from the window."

Another poem by him reads:

Where, I wonder, is he passing the night;

This cold freezing night,
When it is even beginning to storm –
a lonely wayfarer in a world of darkness?

The above poems depict that when man realizes his intimate relationship with nature, his mind becomes full. When a man develops a love of nature he does not care for the worldly possession. This experience throws further light on the concept of happiness. The happiness is the experience of inner richness and fullness which comes from loving experience of reality and cultivating intimate relationship with nature. This transparency and identity established by mystic experience fills the heart and makes a man happy and contented. Thus, the love of nature is not a philosophy to give satisfaction to our sensibility alone, but it provides ontic commitment to nature. The love of nature is according to Zen Buddhism a path to freedom, naturalness and spontaneity. To become natural means to become free and spontaneous in our expressions of feelings. To be natural means to be like a child, a pure and sublime. Child symbolizes the angelic and divine. It is an ignorance that creates artificial barrier's in our mind and keep us away from nature. Natural living, therefore, does not mean returns to natural life of primitive and pre-historic people. It means a life of freedom, emancipation, spontaneity and authentic existence. It means freedom from all conditioning. In this state of artlessness and purposelessness man has have the experience of suchness.

It would be incomplete document if we would not illustrate Japanese love of nature in relation to spirit of Zen Buddhism in the background of the concept and artistic construction of the tea-room or tea-house where the tea ceremony is performed. To take a cup of tea with a friend in such an artistic environment lives the mind above the perplexity and anguish of modern life. The whole idea behind the tea-ceremony is to raise man from the limits of conditionality and give him a glimpse of reality. This deepens the aesthetic sensibility which originates from the mystics understanding of nature.

The Ryokwan was a great lover of trees, a great friend of the louse, of the flea, of the mosquito. He had a tender human feelings for all beings. We would like to state one incident recorded of him is his love for the louse. He used to take great care for the lice by giving it a sun-bath. He has written the following lines in praise of lice:

"O lice, lice
If you were the insects
Singing in the autumn fields,
My chest (fudokori) would really be
For you the Mushasino prairie."

The above lines do not give any philosophical perception of a great truth, but it illustrates the general attitude of the poet towards other forms of life. The uneducated and genuine love for insignificant creatures like lice, has a great significant according to Zen Buddhism, in maintaining the balance and the beauty of biosphere. Though lice is viewed by a common man as an insignificant creature of the universe, but its deliberate extinction would destroy the balance of nature. It would destroy the nature and it would destroy the world. The Zen Buddhism tries to convey this eternal philosophy and truth that, there is a unity in the multiplicity and in the cycle of natural evolution each and every creature which provides a link between the past and the future, between life and death, between appearance and reality is a most significant truth. It is the eternal teaching of the Buddha formulated in his principles of dependent origination. Zen Buddhism advocates Buddhistic ideals and goals through the love of nature.

Notes

1. *Encyclopaedia Britannica*, Vol. XVII, p. 1035.
2. *The World's Living Religions*, p. 222.
3. *Encyclopaedia of Britannica*, Vol. XVI, p. 672.
4. *Zen and Japanese Culture*, pp. 351-52.
5. *Dentoroku* (*Transmission of the Lamp*), p. 27.
6. *Zen and Japanese Culture*, p. 349.
7. *Japan: A Short Cultural History*, p. 392.

CHAPTER 7
The Zen and Confucianism

The Zen and the Confucian Morality

Confucius (K'ung-fu-tsu) was born in 551 B.C. in the state of Lu now a part of Shanting province. His fathers' name was Liang-ko. He was an officer and well-known for his skill, boldness and efficiency. When he attained the ripe old age of 70 Confucius was born. Thus, the Confucius had an old father and young mother. He could not enjoy the love and affection of his father as the later died when he was only 3 years old. His mother had to struggle very hard to rear this young and promising child. It is said that when Confucius was a child he loved to play very much at the arrangements of sacrificial vessels at the end of ceremonies. From his early childhood he used to take keen interest in ceremonies and the process of learning. His formal education started very late. He got his education when he was 15 years old. He was married when he was 19 years old and he was blessed with a son a year after. He started his career as a teacher when he was 22 years old. He used to impart lesson on history and religion. His mother died when he was 28 years old. She was the driving force of his life and it was but natural that he was overtaken by grief and sufferings after the death of his mother. However, he kept himself engaged in pursuit of learning. His scholarship and wisdom attracted a large number of people and his fame spread throughout China. In 516 B.C. Confucius fled away to the neighbouring state of Chi to save his life. However, he could not stay there for longer period and returned to his own province of Lu. He remained unemployed for long 14 years.

Confucius was a great thinker. His political and moral philosophy have had a great impact on all subsequent thinkers of the world. He was the first Chinese thinker who codified ethical and political ideas into concept and theories. Confucianism is an ethical and political philosophy rather than a religious order. He does not spell out any opinion or doctrine on question of religion. However, he considers rites and rituals and ceremonies as important and relevant for moral life. He emphasises on the cultivation of knowledge specially of the natural science. In some of Confucian teachings ethics and ritual have been mingled and assimilated into one. However, his ethical thought and ideas occupy dominant position and hence he is considered as essentially an ethical teacher.

The political philosophy of Confucius is based on the concept of duty relating to filial piety. His universal outlook and his philosophy of universal brotherhood made him a great thinker. He believes that universal brotherhood should be the aims and objects of all corporate life, i.e. family and society. According to him a king has a duty towards his subjects and head of the family towards his family members and neighbours. Thus the concept of the filial piety is the corner stone of his moral and social philosophy. The filial piety is the basis of every corporate life which warrants not only good behaviour of the children towards their parents but also local authority. Confucius believes in the sanctity and coherent of the human relationship, i.e. parent and child, husband and wife, ruler and ruled, which serves as the cementing factor for any corporate life. There is striking similarity between the Confucian ethics and Buddhist *śīla*. Singalovāda of Pāli *Dīghanikāya*[1] expounds in great detail the rights and duties of layman towards his fellow beings, society and state. Both Confucian and Buddhist moral philosophies are based on the wisdom and the virtue of their cultural traditions. However, Confucian teachings are confined to ethical and political issues of daily life of man as a member of a family, state and society. Like the Buddha Confucius also talks little about God and kept mum on supra-natural-being. Like the Buddha Confucius approach to the problem was pragmatic and ethical and this is why both these great thinkers are sometimes called ethical teachers. Manicus (372-389 B.C.), Chushi (A.D. 1130-1200) were the greatest exponents of Confucianism.

Confucius wisdom and knowledge captivated the both ruling elites and the masses of Chinese minds and his teachings created a political upheaval in late second and third century A.D. The intense intellectuals activity and its resultant political awakening forced Chinese mind to accept Confucianism as their official ideology. The whole Chinese political and state craft derived the moral and ethical ideas from him which regulated the behaviours and the social conduct of the ruler and the ruled. However, in the beginning of the third century, Confucianism started waning and lost much of its glory and political appeal because it could not save the empire from schism and disintegration. The Chinese intellectual and the ruling elites became dischanted with Confucianism for some time and started searching new political and moral grounds for the revival of both Chinese empire and social system. In search of new ideals and goals they started revising legalism with its insistence upon hard measure to re-establish law and orders system. These intellectuals started reinterpreting Taoism. However, this intellectual awakening and movement neither re-established Taoism nor rejected Confucianism. In this dialectical movement of thought and ideas Confucianism lost its metaphysical basis and Taoism supplied the philosophical and speculate philosophy to sustain the Chinese philosophical provenance.

This intellectual awakening and movement gave birth to two systems which dominated the intellectual and cultural life of China. One of these two systems put emphasis on the importance of social duties, rituals and the practical affairs of government in maintaining cohesion and progress of both individual and society. This system was the outcome of cultural metamorphosis of Confucianism and legalism and it assumed a new name called "Ming-Chiao" (The doctrine of names). The other system pronounced the importance of Ontological and metaphysical commitment. It considered the quest for permanent behind substratum. Permanent substratum behind the phenomena of change and flux. According to this philosophical tradition there is an impersonal principle which is unlimited, unchanging, indescribable behind all temporarily. This movement imbibed the basic ideas and support both from Taoism and Confucianism and gave birth to a new school of thought known as *Hsuan Hsuch* ("Dark learning").

If we examine the social and cultural life of China we find that Confucianism and Taoism have played most dominant role in creating system of value both political and moral which kept Chinese people together. Confucianism imparted knowledge on social and moral values to define individual's place in society. It helped both individual and the state in maintaining the cooperate life by providing the value system and social reality which bind man with society, husband with wife, state with subjects, ruler with the ruled. Chinese society is one of the most ancient one and it is but natural that there have been innumerable systems of rituals and customs even before the advent of Lao-tze and Confucius. It is evident from all available historical materials and data that Confucianism, Taoism and Buddhism have influenced the Chinese mind and culture and they have kept Chinese philosophical, political, social and cultural traditions alive. These systems are still influencing the Chinese moral system and social conduct. Buddhism played the part of moderating the moral behaviour of Chinese people. Buddhism with its middle path kept the Chinese mind from going astray. It avoids the life of extreme that is the life of indulgence and the life of renunciation. It says that middle path is the only way to deliverance. We can live in the society only through observing the moral and the social conduct. For the observance of moral conduct both the inner urge and external pressure are required. We cannot enforce any moral conduct to people in the absence of inner urge. The inner urge is created by the implicit faith in the system and the pattern of values. This inner urge can be created only by creating a faith in the system. Buddhism with its profound philosophy and doctrines of *Karma* re-birth, *Nirvāṇa* and *Paticcasamuppāda* created faith in life of goodness. *Karma* says: "as you sow, so you will reap." This doctrine creates an earning for moral life to get deliverance and emancipation from the cycle of birth and death. The Chinese society get the moral support both from Confucianism and Buddhism to lead a life of filial piety. On the other hand Confucianism with its political philosophy and doctrine provided the system of external pressure to keep the behaviour of individual within the four walls of political value system.

The Confucianism is concerned with the outer manifestation of human conduct and behaviour whereas Buddhism was more concerned with inner purification of human mind and consciousness and in this way one is complementary to the other. Chinese Buddhism is not the true copy of Indian Buddhism. It blossomed under the moral and the spiritual care of Confucianism and Taoism. It was but natural that Chinese Buddhism assimilated some of the moral teachings and the spiritual teachings of Confucianism and Taoism which resulted into a new form of Chinese Buddhism which is called Ch'an Buddhism or Zen Buddhism.

The Zen Buddhism deeply influenced Neo-Confucianism. The renaissance of Confucian philosophy in Śuṅga Dynasty (960-1279) which is called in Chinese the learning of the Tao was the result of

Zen Buddhism's impact on Chinese philosophy and learning. With the wedlock with Zen Buddhism Confucianism acquired a universal dimension and greater acceptance. The confluence of three religions ushered in the era of creativity and renaissance. The three religions "San Chiao" which became very popular movement during Sang and the Ming Dynasties of China created a composite culture with mixing the Confucian ethics with Taoist System of merits and Buddhist concept of reincarnation. The book of goodness "Shan-Shu" as the Kan-ying Pi-ien ("Tract on Actions and Retribution"). Once the product of these movements of thoughts and ideas known as the schools of three religions. In this renaissance movement both the Confucian and Buddhist followers tried to maintain their identities and purity whereas the followers of Taoism welcome the cultural metamorphosis of three religions. In spite of the initial resistance by followers of Confucianism the process of interaction and mutual understanding continued and the Taoist participation widened the horizon of Chinese mind. In this process of interaction Buddhism was undergone a process "Taoisation" and "Confucianisation" for its adaptation to Chinese conditions. However, the Ch'an Buddhism maintained its philosophical and religious identity because of its profound metaphysical, moral and mystical foundation. Buddhist ideas of purgatory have had a great impact upon Chinese religions. The schools of three religions were ultimately culminated into a new synthesis of thought and practice which is known as Zen Buddhism. Thus, the Ch'an (Zen) Buddhism sheds the alien characters of foreign religion for the Chinese masses and elites and in this way Buddhism was absorbed by Chinese people without any opposition and insistence. The Confucianism created the background by widening the mental horizon of Chinese mind and emphasising the spiritual and philosophical profundity of Buddhism. Humanistic Confucianism worked as catalytic agent for acceptance and assimilation of Buddhism into Chinese culture and way of life. Buddhism on its part provided the Chinese mind a way of life, a spiritual technique to divinise life and attain *Nirvāṇa*. The concept of *Paticcasappāda* and the *Nirvāṇa* bewildered the Chinese creativity and they have been left with no other choice, but to accept it as a way of life, a way of deliverance, and a way of enlightenment.

Confucius formulates his ideas and philosophy similar to those of Lao-tze but he speaks in a different language. In the opening passage of Chung-yung one of the four books presenting the *Confucian*

Philosophy described Taoist ideals as living in accordance with one's own nature. This is called self-realization in Confucian sense. The pursuit of self-realization is called maturation. One cannot disown his own nature. If one can disown his own nature it would mean that, it would not be one's own nature. Therefore, the virtuous man is concerned about himself. According to Confucius the wise man retains his own nature whereas the foolish man does the opposite. The wise man retains his own nature because he is wise and he is wise because he retains his own nature. The foolish man does the opposite because he is a foolish and he is foolish because he fails to appreciate what is good. One's own true nature is self-sufficient, but it is very difficult to maintain it for long. Nature's way is to be genuine and authentic to be genuine and authentic is to act sincerely and truly and without effect which would lead automatically and spontaneously to realize one's own nature. According to Confucius only such man is wise. However, he believes that more self-concern is not sufficient for realizing the fullness of the life. Man is a social being. He finds his expression only through his association with others. According to Confucius a man undisturbed by pleasure, anger or grief or joy is living with his true nature. If he is stimulated by such things as pleasure, anger or grief in its appropriate way he is living with one's own true social nature. This true nature is the primal source from which springs all social affairs. This true social nature is the means for attaining happiness by humanility.

Confucian would greatly emphasise on genuineness. He considers genuineness as self-sufficient. According to him genuineness pervades the whole being of man from beginning to end. Nothing can be attained without genuineness. According to Confucius genuineness is the chief characteristic of a wise man. Genuineness promotes self-realization. It is the means through which one develops his relation with others, self-realization involves associating himself with others. Associating with others creates sympathetic insight and abilities in which one realizes his own nature. One's whole nature (Tao) Integrates both external relation (Social relation) and internal process. According to Confucius genuineness is full, when both of these abilities are appropriately integrated.

Confucius devoted his whole life in observing the practice of various royal societies and studying the records of previous societies, to discover and formulate the most successful ways of organizing human relationship and the attitudes required for conducting a better corporate life. He considers these ideals to imitate others, which made him to recognise as a teacher of customary morality. According to him there are four chief characteristics of a wise man. These are referred to as Yi, Jen, Li and Chih.

1. **Yi:** Yi is the best way of things. We must keep in mind the basic tenet of Lao-tze—that nature and human nature are good. Whenever anything is allowed to live in accordance with its own inner nature all will go well provided, of course, that it does not try to overdo, underdo, or modify it artificially. Yi is the way things behave when they act in accordance with their own natures and this is the best way of all things to act. No man is wise until he understands Yi. He may not completely understand the nature of all things, but he should grasp the fundamental truth that nature provides each being with a nature that is self-sufficient and self-fulfilling and thus as good as it can be. To try to make it better than it is involved trying to change it; trying to change it is artificial; making it artificial will bring it to an unnatural end. Reading Lao-tza's analogy of behaving naturally serves as an excellent background for comprehending the presuppositions underlying Confucius' conception of Yi.

But, since human nature is also essentially social, the best way for human beings to behave is as social beings. What, then, are best ways? What are the principles of social behaviour that each person can discover operating in his own way of doing things? We summarize these under two headings, "the principle of reciprocity" and "the principle of sincerity."

2. **Jen:** Jen means Good will. It is to do what is best for society as we know acting in accordance with one's own nature is best for each person, good will consists basically acting in accordance to one's own nature. A man of good will accepts everyone for what he is. Jen is one's willingness to act according to Yi, Yi is the best way of doing things and Jen good will is willingness to do or to have things done according to one's own nature suited for one's own self and for the society.

Good will is based on the insight and the intimate relationship of inter-dependability. For example a parent wants what is best for his child and wishes him to act according to his own nature. Suppose a parent works very hard to gain his livelihood but would it be proper to expect same hard work from his child? It would be proper for the parent to develop sufficient insight into the nature and capacity of his child. Good will means an insight into the inner strength of others nature and ability to perform action according to one's own nature.

Sympathy is another requirement for the Good will. Not only one must think of other and feels when treated uncertain ways, but one must promote good feelings. Good feelings can emerged only if one has a Good will. The principle of sincerity together with the principle of reciprocity required genuine Good will.

3. **Li:** Li is propriety or the appropriate way of giving overt expressions of inner attitudes. It involves here a basic principle, namely that one's inner nature and one's external behaviour are correlative, or should be correlatives when one's intentions are sincere. Only a deceiver or an ignorance will behave towards others in such a way that they misunderstand his intentions. To act with good intention in a way that others must be sure of your intention that one is conveying his good intention to others, he should in addition, behave in such a way that the other cannot mistake his intention. If there is any other way to convey intentions more clearly and precisely? Yes. At best Confucians concluded from studying the behaviour in different families and courts, both in his own time and as recorded in history. If customs have developed with regard to specific ways of expressing respect, such as bowing, saluting or handshaking one who wishes to be understood will automatically employ these ways. They are the best ways of behaving because they actually convey one's true intention. Hence understanding Yi, the best way of doing things, involves not only having Jen, but also Li or knowing and practicing the best ways or behaving so as to accomplish the intended result.

Once appropriate etiquette has been formalized it becomes the form of civilized life. Also, when parents try to teach their children appropriate manners before they recognise the need for such manners, the children may feel externally forced to conform to a convention that has for them no inner meaning is artificial, not natural and so it is not a part of the best way of doing things. Not only Lao-tze, but Confucius advised us to shun the artificial. But Confucius conceived the artificial behaving in any manner that fails to express inner intentions. For each Yi, the best inner way of behaving, there exists a Li, the most effective external manner of behaving, Li and Yi should be correlated if one seeks his fullest self-realization through his Tao of association. External expression is false unless one both knows Yi and has Jen. Hsin, genuineness requires the desire to be free from all such falsity.

Now, Li may also be called "propriety" or the proper way of behaving. We also speak of this as the "right way" or as "right conduct." Many of us have forgotten that "rite" and "right" have similar meanings and that rituals were originally intended to be the right, i.e. best way of doing things. When social intercourse becomes too complicated for us to keep in mind the value of all social rituals, the later tends to become ritualistic, i.e. forms without meaning. Confucius not only warned against artificially, formalism, or ritualism, but he also sought to discover more detail about right behaviour as social relations became more complicated, as they do in larger families and more intricate systems of government.

4. **Chih:** Chih is wisdom. No man is wise until he is happy. Wisdom consists in confident living. Living confidently involves consenting to things as they are, i.e. to Yi, Jen and Li, three characteristics of the wise man. Wisdom does not require encyclopaedia knowledge. It does not require knowing that allowing each one to act in accordance with his own nature is best for each, and that differences among the natures of the persons upon whom he depends or who depends upon him, must be repeated if he is to live in harmony with them. Achieving Chih requires knowing Yi. If one cannot live confidently until he has, and knows he has, genuine Good will towards others, then he cannot achieve Chih until he fully embodies Jen. If one cannot live confidently until he knows all the appropriate external manners needed to express his true intentions towards others, then he cannot achieve Chih, until he knows and practice Li. Yet merely knowing Yi, having Jen and knowing and practising Li is not enough.

Chih is an ideal to be approached by degrees. One's assurance grows as he learns more one's confidence increases and frees himself fears of inadequacy. One's trust in nature's way—Nature at large, one's own inner nature, and one's social nature — develops as he desires less and less to deviate from their inherent norms. One will achieve Chih fully only when Yi, Jen and Li have become embodied within him so completely that the responds in each occasion social aid private, with perfect spontaneity. In Chih, one lives according to habit, without question or reservation. *Chih* involves *hsin*. Complete unwillingness to deceive oneself or others? *Chih* epitomises *yea*-saying, thereby making the ideals of Confucius among the greatest religious ideals of all mankind. It is Confucius's ideal of *Chih* that makes Confucianism a great religion and not the deification of Confucius by latter admirers nor his teachings about "ancestor worship." *Chih* is wisdom because a person having achieved it responds to his opportunities and responsibilities, so unreservedly, so automatically and spontaneously, that he never for a moment abandons the habit of living confidently. *Chih* is such a high religious ideal that Confucius himself complained that he was never able to reach it even though he tried his best throughout his life.

Confucius did believe in ancestor worship. Question arises whether be recommended specific ways for revering ancestors? Yes. Did he believe in the continued existence of departed ancestors in some incorporeal form? To this question, as to questions about the existence of spirit of any kind, he gave a positive answer. His reply is "Not know life, how know death?" Why, then, should he have bothered so much about specific ways of revering ancestors? You already know the answer if you can apply *Yi*, *Jen* and *Li* to your relations with your own ancestors.

Consider, for example, how the principle of reciprocity applied here. Do you expect to die and become a departed ancestors? Yes. Do you desire to be forgotten as soon as die? No. How long do you desire to be remembered after you are dead? Should you not then according to the principle of reciprocity, desire to remember your ancestors in the same way as you desire to be remembered when you become one? How should you express your remembrance of the goodness and greatness of your ancestors? In the same manner you desire to be so remembered. Since, you doubtless do not wish to be forgotten too soon, specially by those dearest to you, nor remembered too long, especially by those who were never acquainted with you. You may find some socially accepted and culturally established manner of enacting such a remembrance.

Thus, what appears to others as superstitions ancestor worship was for Confucius a natural expression of self-respect by social and individuals. When we recognize additionally that one's social *Tao* involves *Hsin* or sincerity we will then want to remember our ancestors as sincerely as we desire to be remembered. Do our ancestors still really exist? The principles of reciprocity and seniority require that we regard our ancestors as existing in the same way in which we now desire others to regard us as existing after we have become departed ancestors. The naturalness of this desire makes it appropriate to set-up Tombstones, memorial days, tablets, halls, gardens, ceremonies etc. which flow from our nature as social beings.

Confucius did not regard man as victims of determinate process of nature. Men become agencies that help to determine the course of nature, but it is only to be who is completely genuine in the affairs of this world who can develop his nature to its fullest. If he can develop his own nature to its fullest, then he can help in the full development of other man's nature, then he can help in the full development of the nature of all animate and inanimate beings. If he can help in the full development of the nature of all animate and inanimate beings then he can help in the production and maturation activities of nature above and nature below. When he helps in the production and maturation activities of nature above and below, be becomes a third kind of agency in the universe.

Confucius was not only a great teacher but he was a man of practical wisdom also. When he attained the age of fifty he was appointed as ruler of the middle district known as *Chung-tu* of the province of *Li*. He proved to be a very successful administration. His fame as an administrator travelled far and wide and he was raised to the position of the minister of public work. His devotion to his duty and his high ideals made him the minister of justice. In his last year of public service he became acting chancellor. The administration of Confucius is a high watermark of Chinese history of government. It is said that, after Confucius conducted the government of state for three months, the seller of the lambs and other articles off no longer falsifier their prices. When man and woman walked on different side of the road lost objects were not pick up on the street. Stranger who came from all sides did not need any help from the police and the official for him entering the city because they were received with warm and sincerity and they had the feeling that they are returning to their own homes.[2]

The success of Confucius became a matter of great concern for the people of neighbouring state of *Chi*. They started thinking that the state of *Lu* under the administration of Confucius would occupy a dominant position and hence, they started conspiring against Confucius and his state. They presented *Duke-ting* who appointed Confucius as the minister of justice with an eighty beautiful dancing girls and a hundred and twenty magnificent horses in order to divert his mind from policies to pleasure. The prince was made victim of the conspiracy and he started taking little interest in government and important ceremonial sacrifices. This came as a great shock to Confucius and he left the government. He attained by now sixty six years of age. After the departure from the government the life of hardship and the fourteen years of wandering started. He left Lu and was wondered in *Chi* given out of *Śuṅga* and *Wei* and suffered want and humiliations between *Chen* and *Ts'sai*. After this long wondering and hardship he returned to his own state *Lu*. It is said that Confucius was nine feet six inches tall. All the people called him giant. He was received with warm and sincerity to his own state of *Lu*. However, the government did not make any use of Confucius wisdom and administrative experiences. Neither Confucius strived for any official position. After that he devoted his whole soul in literary activities and teachings. He was a great hard task master and in spite of his severe instruction he gathered around him some three thousands students for whom he imparted knowledge in the odes, records, rites and music. However, in his everyday life he was a modest. In the ancestral temple and at court he was eloquent. At court he used to converse with the higher dignitaries in definite terms and to the point. And with the lower dignitaries he was clear and open. When he used to enter at the prince door he used to bow over and with quick steps. Whenever prince ordered his presence at the reception of guest he used to be very serious. Such was the period of his last years. In the last moment of his anguish he said "Alas no one knows me." When he was asked to clarify and elucidate his above statement he said he did not have murmur against heaven. He harbours no ill-will against man. His anguish is best explained in the following lines which he uttered during his last illness:

> "The Sacred Mountain caves in,
> The roof beam breaks,
> The sage will vanish."

After that he wept and said to Tzekung one of his disciple that, the world had been ill-governed for long time. People would not understand him. He narrated his dream and said, that he was sitting before sacrificial offerings between the two pillars. After seven days Confucius die at the age of seventy three years. Confucius was buried north of the city at the bank of river—Szu and that marked the closer of one of the most brilliant chapter of life of learning and noble teaching. His disciples mourned the death of their great teacher for three years. When after three years of mourning they separated and went their ways and started going their own ways once again they started weeping. Such was the impact of Confucius on his disciples. The seeing of departure of Confucius strikes the similarity of the Buddha leaving the world and entering into the state of *Mahāpari-nirvāṇa.* It is said when the Buddha was departing even the inanimate objects like trees and flowers were taken with grief and the birds and the animals mourning on the passing away of the Buddha. Some of the disciples of Confucius built their huts near to the grave. They were hundred families of the disciples of Confucius and of the people of Lu who built their houses near to the grave and they called the place the hamlet of Confucius. In Lu the custom was handed down from generation to generation to offer sacrifices at the grave of Confucius at the fix time of the year. There was a custom to hold archery contest at the grave of Confucius and scholars used to practice the rites of communal banquet. The burial place of Confucius is one hundred acres in extent. The hall in which disciples of Confucius used to live was later turned into a temple in which the cloths, hats and books of Confucius were preserved. All of them were kept for over two hundred years until the Hang dynasty. The first Emperor of Hang dynasty offered great sacrifice to Confucius when he was passing through Lu. This was the customary practice to first visit the temple the princess, ministers and high officials whenever they used to visit Lu. Some thinkers say that Confucius was basically agnostic in religion. The basis of their such observation is Confucius advised to keep aloof from the spirits. He meant thereby that one should maintain a safe distance from the spirits. Kuhung-Ming translates the statement of Confucius as such. "To know the essential duties of man living in a society of men, and to hold in fear and awe the spiritual powers of the universe, while keeping aloof from irrelevant familiarity with them, that may be considered as understanding."

However, Confucius deepest interest was in the essential duties of man living in society. He devoted major part of his life on reflecting on the problem of organization of society in accordance with ethical principles. He did not claim as the advocate of this principles but transmits of this knowledge which headed down out of hoary past. The following quotation will through light on the basic teachings and attitude of Confucius.

The master said, "I have transmitted what was taught to me without making up anything of my own." I have been faithful to and loved the ancients... I have never grown tired of learning nor wearied of teaching others what I have learnt.

The Duke of Shu asked Tsu-lu about master King. Tzu-lu did not reply. The Master said, why did you not say "This is the character of the man so intent upon enlightening the younger that he forgets his hunger, and so happy in doing so, that he forgets the bitterness of his lot and does not realize that old age is at hand. That is what he is."

The Master said, I for my part am not one of those who have innate knowledge. I am simply one who loves the past and who is diligent in investigating it.

The Master said, at fifteen I set my heart upon learning. At thirty, I had planted my feet firm upon the ground. At forty, I no longer suffered from perplexities. At fifty, I knew what were buildings of Heaven. At sixty, I heard them with docile ear. At seventy, I could followed the dictates of my own heart; for what I desire no longer, overstepped the boundaries of right.

The Master said, it is goodness that give to a neighbourhood its beauty. One who is free to choose, yet does not prefer to dwell among the good—how can be accorded the name of wise?

The Master said, without goodness a man—

> Cannot for long endure adversity,
> Cannot for long enjoy prosperity.

The good man rest content with goodness; he that is merely wise pursues goodness into believe that it pays to do so.

There is an old adage, "Only a good nan knows how to like people knows how to dislike them", the Master said, he whose heart is in the smallest degree set-upon goodness well dislike no one.

The Master said, in the morning, here the way, in the evening die content.

The Master said, in the presence of a good man, think all the time how you may learn to equal him. In the presence of a bad man, turn your gaze within.

The Master said, he who will not worry, about what form of will soon find something worse than worry close at hand.

The Master said, the gentleman who takes the right and his material to work upon and ritual as the guide in putting what is right into practice who is modest in setting out his projects and faithful in carrying them to their conclusion, he indeed is a true gentleman.

The Master said, a gentleman is distressed by his own lack of capacity. He is never distressed at the failure of others to recognize his merits. The master said, a gentleman has reason to be distressed if he ends his days without making a reputation for himself.

The Master said, the demands that a gentleman makes are upon himself. Those that a small man makes one upon others.

The Master said, a gentleman is polite, but not quarrelsome to allies himself with individuals, but not with parties.

> The Master said, A gentleman does not
> Accept man because of what they say,
> Not reject saying, because the speaker is what he is.

Tzu-Kung asked saying, Is there any single saying that one can act upon all day and everyday? The Master said, perhaps the saying about consideration : "Never do to others what you would not like them to do to you."[3]

Confucius believes that society can be put to order through the cultivation of the self. According to him the way of learning consists in the cultivation of self and moral personality. This cultivation of self and moral personality creates new people who would abide in highest goodness. To know one's abiding place leads to fixity of purpose. Fixity of purpose to calmness of mind, calmness of mind to serenity of life, serenity of life, to careful consideration of means, careful consideration of means to the achievement of the end.

Confucius has dealt in great detail about human affairs and moral conduct of people. He says that things have their roots and branches and human affairs have their ending as well as beginning to know what comes first and what comes afterwards leads one to near the way the health of a nation begins from the health of individual and the family. If you want to have a great society you would have to govern your own states efficiently. To govern your state efficiently you should maintain harmony in your own family. To maintain the harmony in the family you will have to cultivate your own individual self. To cultivate your own self you should put your mind in proper place, to put your mind right you must have to cultivate genuine purpose. The cultivation of genuine purpose and accumulation of knowledge consists in appreciating the nature of things. According to Confucius the knowledge culminates in the appreciation of nature and in the culmination of knowledge purpose becomes genuine. With genuine purpose the mind becomes right, with right mind individual self-blossoms with the flowering of the self-family becomes a happy home, with the establishment of the harmony the state is governed efficiently. The efficient government heralds the emergence of a great society, the great society is at peace under the good government. According to Confucius if the above rules of good government and moral conduct are observed, then from the son of heaven down to the common people enjoy, harmony, peace and unity. The flowering of the individual self is at the root of the great society, and benevolent state.

On analysis of Confucius doctrines of "mean" we come to the following moral teachings:

> "The way is not far removed from man. If a man pursues a way which removes him from men, he cannot be in the way... The treatment which you do not like for yourself you must not hand out to others."

There are five things according to Confucius which are the basis of a great society. They are the relationship between sovereign and subject between father and son, between husband and wife, between elder and younger brother and the equal intercourse of friends and friends. These five relationships constitute great society. Knowledge, human heartedness and fortitude are the means of the growing and emergence of great society as these qualities are the spiritual power which bind society into one whole.

That which heaven entrust man is to be called his nature. To cultivate one's own nature is called the way. The cultivation of way is to be called instruction of systematic truth. One must not abandon even for a moment the way. The way keeps man restrain and keyed up in relation to the unseen world. A man of principle remains on guard when he is along with himself. Confucius says, "To have no emotions of pleasure and anger and sorrow and joy surging up. This is to be described as being in a state of equilibrium. To have these emotions surging up but all tune, this is to be described as a state of harmony. This state of equilibrium is the supreme foundation. This state of harmony is a sign of the Great society. Once equilibrium and harmony are achieved, heaven and earth maintain their proper positions, and all living things are nourished."[4]

After the death of Confucius China was in grip in warring State in which various political units wanted to stablish their supremacy over others. It was also a period in which numerous others philosophical schools arose to compete with Confucianism. In past for hundred years or so Confucianism seemed to become weaker rather than stronger. After hundred years of the death of Confucius many divergent schools of thoughts came into existence which was referred as the doctrines of the hundred schools. However, due to the scholarship and work of Confucius devoted disciples Méncius and Hsuntzu Confucianism came out victorious and it established its superiority over others. Mencius advocated the principles of benevolence. Mencius joined issues with utilitarianism of Motu. He was strong believer in essential goodness of man and therefore, he thought the practice of virtue is a necessary expression of human nature. To illustrate Mencius believe of fundamental goodness of human nature we may recite his famous saying which he argued that "man tends to seek good just as water tends to rundown bill." The statement was made in opposition to a contrary statement by little known philosophers named Kautzu. Kautzu said our nature is like whirlpool; if a bridge is made to the east the water flow west. If the bridge is made to the west it flows to the west. As water does not discerns between east and west man's nature does not discern between good and evil. Mencius said that the water does not discern between east and west, but does it not discern between up and down? Man's nature will be good as water flows dawn. No man but is good. No water but flows down. If you hit water and make it leap you can send it above your forehead; force it and you can bring it up a hill. But is that the nature of water? It is done by force. And when a man is brought to do evil, the same is done to his nature. To give a glimpse of Mencius... interpretation of Confucianism we would quote the following passages.

> "Mencius said, The great man is he that does not lose the child heart. Mencius said, Man's heart is love, man's road is right. To leave the road unfollowed, (to) let me heart stray and not know where to see it, is sad indeed.
> If a man's dog or hen strays, he knows where to seek it; but when his heart strays he knows not where to seek it. The scholar's way is no more than seeking our stray heart."[5]

Mencius developed the Confucianism and made it more popular whereas Hsun-tau systematised the Confucian teachings and made it school of thought. Hsun-tzu transformed the Confucianism into a naturalistic humanism. He de-personalised the concept of heaven and spirit of Confucianism and conceived it as naturalistic law. Man was, therefore, cast upon his own resources and challenge to do his utmost to achieve progress through his own unaided effort. He said that, prosperity and calamity did not come from heaven. According to him heaven has a constant regularity of action. The fix stars make the round the sun and the moon alternatively shine. The four seasons come in succession and this the movements of stars are no more secret. However, we do not know the invisible source that is what is meant by the work of heaven according to Confucius. The wise man is he who is anxious and plan about what is within his power and does not seek for what comes from heaven. If a man neglects what he can do and he seeks for what heaven does he fails to understand the nature of things, with this systematization of Confucius Doctrines by Mencius and Hsun-tzu, it became a philosophical school and political doctrines and re-established its superiority over others. A vigorous new Confucian school arose which maintained that the solution of the social and the political problems was to be found in the teachings of classical antiquity. Shun-shi was undoubtedly the greatest of the new Confucius's who played dominant role in formulation of Confucianism and transforming it as a school of natural humanism which was accepted by the Chinese mind without any resistance and reservation.

To understand Confucius it is desirable to visualize the state of affairs of his time. His doctrine was of this worldly social mindedness. His interest in political administration of affairs was dry and unromantic, because of the fact that he lived in an environment where the chaos reigned there was a little respect for law and order. The whole society was in the state of chaos and disarray. Aristocracy used to amused in hunting, war and extravagant living which led great burden on the common mass. Before the advent of Confucius there was only one school of archery. He was the first who started imparting knowledge without any class distinction. It was the gift of Confucius who abolished any qualification of birth as necessary criteria for administrative and diplomatic assignment. Thus, he laid the foundation of the modern bureaucratic system. According to him whoever has the capacity and ambition for learning and becoming scholar and to serve his state he should be given opportunity, irrespective of his social position and family background. He was thus one of the greatest teacher and educator that the world has witnessed.

To make education free from all restrictions of various social and political class was undoubtedly a great revolution. It is debatable point as to what extend democratic ideas can be attributed to Confucius as there is a close sociological relation between democracy and the natural sciences. There are some thinkers who consider Confucius as a great counter revolutionary.

Confucius seems to have believe that the true aim of Government ought to be the welfare and the happiness of the whole people. He was of the opinion that it would be brought about not by enactment of arbitrary law, but by subtle administration generally accepted and having the sanction of natural law. He believed that the man of learning sympathy intelligence and goodness be made the helm of state affairs for the betterment and welfare of the people. He was quite sanguine that ability to govern has no necessary relation with birth, wealth and social position. According to him capacity to administer society depends on character and knowledge which comes through right education. He believed in the universal education. This was the most revolutionary concept and great contribution of Confucius.

From his concept of education many important conclusions were derived. If every man is potentially educable then every man is potentially as good judge of truth as every others. What matters in making a man good administrator and good moral being is the qualification which add value to his judgement through the process of education and experience.

The group of Confucius understood this intellectual democracy. Confucius himself often caused suspended judgement saying that one should leave on one side what is doubtful and that scribes should follow the good old practice of living a blank space in text when copying, instead of taking a character of which they were not sure.

Confucius says: "Shall I tell you what knowledge is, when you know a thing to say that you know it; when you do not know a thing to admit that you do not know it—this is true knowledge." This is the basis of any modern scientific academy. Confucius's accommodation to study the Book of Odes was to widen own acquaintance with names of birds, bees, plants and trees. Confucius did believe in the moral order of the universe, but he also made use of the Tao way of not for any other purpose, but for the ideal way the order of human society. He did not made distinction and separated man from social man or social man from whole nature because he considered proper study of mankind was man.

The Confucian agnostic rationalism made a sharp attack on the prevalent superstitious believe and the practices of the then Chinese life. With the development of Confucianism under the influence and impact of Taoism and Buddhism it developed into an organic view of the world in the beginning. In the early Confucianism there was no distinction between ethics and politics. The government was paternalistic. The early Confucianists believe that a prince was virtuous people. There was no equivocation about the concept of virtue peace and justice. The early Confucianists developed a doctrine of names that is doctrine of actions and relations. This doctrine advocated the right of rebellions against the unchristian princes which is considered as the profound contribution of sixteenth and seventeenth century theologians. The right of revolt against unethical and tyrannical rules of the princes was conceived and formulated as political doctrine by early Confucian school. The Confucian bureaucracy was considered as best form of administrative system conceived by any thinker as it was made to champion the causes of the people. The democratic elements in Confucianism was in abundance and real. To clarify the democratic elements we cite the following passages.

Chi-Khang Tzu asked Master Kuang about the art of ruling. The Master said, Ruling (Cheng, governing) is a straightening (Cheng rectifying). If you lead along a straight way, who will dare go by a crooked one.

Chi-Khang Tzu was troubled by robbers. He asked Master Khung what he should do. Master Khung replied, if only you were free from desires they would not steel even you paid them to.

Chi-Khang Tzu asked the master about government, saying, “Supposing we liquidated all those people who have not that the Tao in order to help those who do have the Tao, what would you think of it?” The Master Khung replied, “You are there to rule, not to kill. If you desire what is good, the people will be good. The Chun-Tzu has the virtue of wind, the people have the virtue of grass. The grass must needs bend when the wind blows over it.”

Tzu-Yu (Yen Yen) said, formerly, Master, I heard you, say,

"When the Chun-tzu learns well the Tao, he loves man. When the Hsiao-tzen learns well the Tao, he is easily led."

Duke-Ting, asks if there were anyone phrase that sufficed to save a country. Master Khung replied, "No phrase could ever be like that. But there is one that comes near to it." There is a saying among men, "It is hard to be a prince and not easy to be a minister." A ruler no really understood that it was hard to a prince would have come fairly near to saving his country by a single phrase. Duke-Ting said, "Is there anyone phrase, that could ruin a country?" Master Khung replied, "No phrase could ever be like that. But there is one that comes near it. There is a saying among men: "What pleasure is there in being prince unless one can say whatever one chooses and no one dare to disagree?" So long as what he says is good, it is of course also good that he should not be opposed. But, if what he says is bad, will it not come near to ruining his country by single phrase?

From the above passages it is clear that Confucius believed that man was born of uprightness. If he loses it and yet he lives it is the effect of more good fortune. These issues kept the Chinese mind engaged for considerable period. On one side Confucianism was basically rationalistic and opposed to any superstitious or even super natural form of religion. On the other side it intends concentration of interest upon human social life to the exclusion of non-human phenomena negated the scientific enquiry and explanation it is not only in China to prove that rationalism was less favourable than mysticism to the progress of science. Confucianism favoured traditional rites and ceremonies and it remains sceptical and averse to true religious thought and practices. Confucius had no intention of being got involved into discussion of such phenomena which have had no bearing on the problems of human society. His followers adhered to the principles of his master to the despair of Taoist and technologists for nearly two thousand years. Needham observed Confucianism as a "religion" had no theologians who could resent the intrusion of the scientific view of the world into their preserves. It simply turned away its face, in accordance with the attitude of its founding fathers, from nature and the investigation of nature, to concentrate a millennial interest on human and human society alone."[6]

Śuṅga Dynasty is considered as the trouble age in the history of China. But it gave a philosophy which is the flower of the Chinese mind. The philosophy attained a monumental development during this period. The speculative mind of China paint up during the Han and succeeding dynasties blossomed under the pressure of an alien power, into a sublime philosophy. This flowering of the Chinese philosophy assimilated in itself the alien philosophy Buddhism and syncretised and formulated on the basis of Chinese creativity. The teaching of Zen Buddhism which opened new vistas and a new schools of thoughts. When Confucianism turned into a more study of rituals and the practice of social morality and as a result it lost its mooring and roots Buddhism saved it from total collapse of Chinese creativity. Taoism was already buried under its own superstitious believes and could not inspire religious practice. There was nothing to revitalise the intellectual and the creative Chinese mind by infusing new and fresh blood of thought into Confucianism. If Zen Buddhism would not have ushered at the critical juncture of intellectual crisis of Chinese mind with its profound philosophy and meditative technique of enlightenment Chinese would not have lived philosophically. Almost all the thinkers of the Śuṅga Dynasty at least once in their lives have been the active practiceners of Zen. After coming close contact with Zen philosophy and meditative practice the Chinese minds started revaluating their own philosophies born out of their own soil. The Śuṅga philosophy was the outcome of their spiritual adventures. Though the Chinese mind started denouncing Buddhism and Buddhist method of meditative practice they were already accepted Buddhist philosophy and way of life in their inner most heart.

The Zen monks were on the other hand students of Confucianism and as Stubborn Chinese they could not be anything else the difference between Confucian scholars and the Zen-masters was that the Confucian based their philosophy on the native system while Zen Buddhists adhered to the basic teachings of Buddhism as enunciated by *Bodhi Dharma*, but they started speaking Buddhism in Confucian language. The Zen monks interpreted Confucian texts in Buddhistic way and they commented on Buddhist literature from the Confucian point of view. The Zen Buddhism, Confucianism and Taoism were assimilated into one philosophy which is known as Śuṅga philosophy. D.T. Suzuki says: "Suffice it to state here that Zen is, in fact, the Chinese way of responding to Indian thought and represented by Buddhism and that, this being so, Zen, as it developed in the Tang and later flourished in the Śuṅga, could be nothing else, but a reflection of Chinese mentality—by which I mean it was eminently practical and ethical. In this respect, there was very probability of Zen's taking on Confucian colouring. But in the beginning of Zen's history its philosophy was Indian, that is, Buddhistic, for there was nothing corresponding to it in the traditional teaching of Confucianism. And this was the element the later Confucian thinkers consciously or unconsciously wished to incorporate into their own system."[7] In short Zen adopted the practical teachings of Confucian morality and social reality and Confucianism absorbed the abstract speculation of Buddhism which provided metaphysical foundation to the waning teaching of Confucianism. It was a normal practice for the Zen monks to become advocates of Confucianism in addition to preaching Buddhism. We do not agree with D.T. Suzuki's observation that Zen Buddhism does not have philosophy of its own.[8] Dr. Suzuki has made a contradictory statements about Zen Buddhism. At one place he says, that Zen Buddhism provided a metaphysical foundation to the teaching of Confucian and at the same time he says strictly speaking Zen has no philosophy of its own.[9] Zen Buddhism has a profound metaphysical basis which provided infrastructure for both the Confucianism and Taoism. It is another fact that Zen Buddhists are sometimes Confucianists sometimes Taoists and sometimes even Shintōists. This explains the universal philosophical outlook and the mystical basis of Buddhism which can even be adopted and explained by Western religious experience.

In the fourteenth and the fifteenth century the five mountains that is the five Zen monasteries were in Kyoto. They were in publishing headquarters of Confucian scriptures. Zen monks without any reservation and inner restrictions used to edit and print the text books of both Buddhism and Confucianism. The activities of Zen monks were not confined to the teachings of Buddhism alone. They were for all practical purposes—Buddhist's turned to Confucianists and Confucianists turned to Buddhists. Of the Zen-masters mention may be made of the Muso the national teachers (1275-1351), Genye (1269-1352), Kokwan Shiren (1278-1346), Chugan Yengetsu (1300-1375), Gido Shushin (1321-1388), and others all of whom propagated and popularized the study of Confucian classic in accordance with the spirit of Zen Buddhism. It was a customary practice that even the Emperor Shogus used to practice Zen Buddhism and at the same time they used to attend the Zen-masters' lectures on Confucianism. The Emperor Hanazono (Reigned — 1308-1317) was a sincere scholar of Śuṅga School of Chinese philosophy and earnest practitioner of Zen Buddhism. His statue, in the robes of a Zen monks sitting of cross-legged in serene dignity, it still preserved in his room at Myoshing ji where he used to sit in meditation. His residence which was presented to his Zen teacher Kwanzan (1277-1360) became the foundation of the present Myoshin ji the most powerful branch of *Rinzai*-sect in the western part of Kyoto, Japan.

As we have already stated in previous Chapters that, Zen is neither a concept nor a religion. It is a way of life and spiritual experience which deliver man from the snares of subjective illusion and objective miseries. Zen has nothing to do with nationalism as it is neither an institutionalized religion nor the denominational in character. It is a technique of meditational practice which leads to enlightenment. However, when Zen first came to Japan from China, it was steeped in Confucianism. It was but natural that Zen was not advocated in Japan in its pure form, free from the cultural metamorphosis and transfigures. It is a fact of history that Japanese mind did not accept Zen Buddhism with everything that came along with it. There are two original traditions of Chinese cultural life that is Confucianism and Taoism which got amalgamated and assimilated into Zen Buddhism. Confucianism is famous for its practicality and positivism, whereas Taoism is representative of mysticism and speculative trends. When Buddhism entered into China during Hang Dynasty (A.D. 64) it got associated with the philosophy of Lao-tze and Chung-tze. In the beginning Buddhism was not taken very seriously by Chinese elites and the masses. The early followers of Buddhism were mostly engaged in translating Buddhist texts into Chinese, but after going through the Chinese version of Buddhist texts, creative Chinese mind was captivated and they found Buddhist philosophy not only very inspiring but profound and sublime. With the rendering of the *Prajñāpāramitā Sūtra* into Chinese the study of Buddhism was taken with all seriousness though in the beginning Chinese mind could not comprehend the concept of *Śūnyatā*, however, they could found it somewhat similar to Lao-tzuan concept of Wu (nothingness). At this period of Chinese history Kumārajīva appeared in China with his profound scholarship and persuasive mind. He was one of the most brilliant *Ācārya* of Buddhist tradition who visited China to propagate the philosophy and the religion of Śākyamuni. He translated many *Mahāyāna* texts into Chinese and he attracted many disciples who became devoted and dedicated to the cause of spreading Buddhism in China. The San-Lun school of Buddhism was established in China by Cohi-stang (548-623), who based his teachings on the *Mahāyāna* philosophy of Nāgārjuna. The profound and the sublime philosophy of Nāgārjuna created intellectual upsurge and spiritual awakening in the land of Confucius and Lao-tze. The San-Lun school was followed by the T'ien-t'ai (*tendai*), Wei-shih (*yuishiki*), and the Hua-yen (*kegon*) in the Sui and the T'ang Dynasties. The T'ien-t'ai is based on the *Saddharmapuṇḍarika*, the Wei-shih on the idealistic teaching of Asaṅga and Vasubandhu, and the Hua-yen on the philosophy of the infinite as expounded in the Avataṁsaka. The philosophy of the infinite and the indescribability of nature of reality expounded in *Avataṁsaka sūtra* of Buddhist scripture received great attention and appreciation by Chinese mind. It is considered as the high watermark of speculative and religious mind of Chinese Buddhism. It was the creative genius of Chinese mind that it could assimilated and digested the profound teaching of *Avataṁsaka sūtra*. The different trends and traditions of Buddhist philosophy specially the teachings of Nāgārjuna and the deep philosophical insight of *Avataṁsaka sūtra* awakened the Chinese mind from its long slumber and paved the path for the flowering of Śuṅga philosophy.

With the blossoming of the Śuṅga philosophy, Chinese mind underwent intellectual transformation. At this very period of Chinese creativity *Bodhidharma* appeared at the religious life of China. With his tremendous spiritual power deep philosophical insight and foresight he became a renaissance man of new Buddhism called as Zen Buddhism. D.T. Suzuki says: "Zen appealed partly to the empirical proclivity of Chinese mentality and partly to its craving for mysticism. Zen despised learning of letters and upheld the intuitive mode of understanding, for its followers were convinced that this was the most direct and effective instrument with which to grasp ultimate. In fact, empiricism and mysticism and positivism can walk hand in hand quite readily. They all look for the facts of experience and are shy of building up an intellectual framework around them."[10]

However, a man is a social being also he cannot remain satisfy with mere spiritual experience alone. Man wants to share his experience with others. To share one's own intuitive experience it must have its contents and metaphysical ideas to support his experience when one start questioning his own thought and experience. Zen Buddhism formulated his whole philosophy on the basis of spiritual experience and hence it remained confine to the intuitive plan of understanding. It met the best use of metaphors, symbols and poetic imagination, but it could not provide metaphysical foundation for its spiritual experience. The assimilation of Hua-Yen (Kegon) philosophy with Zen Buddhism became pronounced in the teaching of Ch'eng Kuan (Chokwan 738-838) and Tsung-mi (Shumitsu, 780-841). These two great Chinese intellectuals and teachers were followers of both the schools of Hua and Zen Buddhism. It was through this process of assimilation of thoughts that Zen Buddhism started influencing the Confucian school of thought. Though the disciples of Confucians like Chu-Hsi and his followers Chou Tun-I (Shu-Ton-i, 1017-1073) and Ming-tao (Meido, 1085-1139), started with missionary zeal to re-establish philosophy on purely Chinese thought, they derived great inspiration from the "Four Books." However, their study of the Zen Buddhism had played great impact on the formulation of Confucian thought and ideas as it is evident in the concept of sudden illumination which was definitely an alien concept. The concept of primordial substance U-chi or Tai-chi was the contribution of *Mahāyāna* Buddhism to Chinese ontology and cosmogony. The non-dual nature of reality as advocated by *Mādhyamikā* and the theory of no origination of Nāgārjuna and the concept of *Nirvāṇa* paved the path for the emergence of *Advaita* thought in the philosophy of Śuṅga school. The Śuṅga school of thought was decidedly rooted in its native culture and tradition and at the beginning they had no stomach for Buddhist philosophy because of its denial of materiality of the world. Chinese mind has empirical bias and it always upheld the world of particularities. Chinese are basically patriotic and a nationalistic race. They have preference for positivism than idealism. They are earthly people though sometimes they may stair at stars and get lost into the stupendous beauty of the celestial world. The down to earth approach of the Zen-masters and their practical wisdom attracted the Chinese mind and it made great contribution in blossoming the new School of Śuṅga philosophy.

Fujiwara Seikwa (1561-1619) and Razan (1583-1657) were the first official exponents of Śuṅga philosophy in Japan. Seikwa was Buddhist monk, but the study of Confucianism was played such an impact that he cast off his Buddhist robe though he retained his shaven head for some time. In course of time Confucianism Shintōism and Buddhism were syncretised and got embedded in Japanese mind. Zen Buddhism played great role in synthesising Confucianism, Taoism and Shintōism into religio-nationalistic dialectic of Japanese cultural life.

The Zen and the Down to Earth Philosophy

Zen Buddhism was accepted as a way of life by Chinese mind because of its down to earth philosophy. Buddhism got its entry into China in the turn of the first century, but it could not make much impact on the creative mind of Chinese in the beginning. The Chinese had a natural dislike for the monks who did not work for their living, but went on begging for their food. They had natural disapproval who did not marry and who did not have any offsprings to own their memories and affections in proper Confucian way. However, the *Mahāyāna* Buddhist scriptures particularly *Prajñāpāramitā Sūtra*, *Laṅkāvatāra Sūtra*, *Mādhyamikā-kārikā* of Nāgārjuna, *Abhidhamma Kośa* of Vasubandhu and *Avamaṁsaka Sūtra* captivated the creature imagination of Chinese minds because of their profound philosophy and spiritual depth contained in the above Buddhist literatures. In spite of the initial opposition and apathy of the Chinese scholars towards Buddhism, scholars and *Ācārya* of great merits and spiritual attainments continued visiting China with the sole mission of propagating the lofty ideals and the philosophy of deliverance from suffering and assured method of salvation of Lord Buddha. By the sixth century A.D. these Buddhist *Ācāryas* and teachers established many schools of Buddhism in China which created tension and opposition by the followers of Confucius and Lao-tze.

Whether it was an accident of history or a dialectic expressed in time of Bodhidharma suddenly appeared at the intellectual horizon of China and kept the Chinese mind dazzled with his deep philosophical wisdom and tremendous esoteric powers which he attained during uninterrupted practice of Buddhist meditation for nine long years gazing the wall. There is no agreement amongst the historians about his life and teachings in China. However, from one account he was son of a king of Kāñjīvaram in South India. He got imitation in *Dhyāna* Buddhism from his teacher Prajñatara and he was conferred the title of Twenty Eighth Patriarch of *Dhyāna* Buddhism, He left India after the death of his teacher and reached China at the time of Emperor Wu in 520 A.D. The emperor was a devout Buddhist. His spiritual encounter with Bodhidharma had a great impact on the mind of Emperor and made him realized the uselessness of Buddhist rituals and believe which did not have any direct bearing on the experience of *Satori*. Emperor said to Bodhidharma with the sense of great attainment that he had built many temples and monasteries, studied

Buddhist scriptures and even rendered them into Chinese and converted many laymen in Buddhist religious order and he was instrumental in making them into monks. After narrating his above so-called religious and moral achievements he enquired what was his merits? Bodhidharma replied to His Majesty's enquiry threw this Majesty's mind out of track and created tremendous starred in His Majesty's whole being. The Emperor made second enquiry about the first principle of the *Dharma*. "The vast emptiness and nothing holy therein" was the reply of Zen-master. Emperor asked "who then to confront me?" "I do not know" said Bodhidharma and he entered into cave for meditation. He transmitted his knowledge to the Chinese patriarch. He imparted his knowledge to his disciples stating that each one had Buddhahood and the essence of Buddha-mind. He was speaking from his no-mind.

Zen teachings and philosophy can be summarized in following sentences:

> "A special transmission outside the scriptures,
> Not depending upon the letter,
> But pointing directly to the mind,
> And leading us to see into the Nature itself,
> Thereby making us attain Buddhahood."

Zen claims to be a special transmission outside the scriptures. If we analyse the philosophical meaning of the above statement it simply conveys that Zen Buddhism does not belong to the religio-philosophical schools of Buddhism. But it belongs to the esoteric and tantric tradition of Buddhism which do not believe in the philosophical abstractions and conceptualization. Zen does not attach any credence to concept and rational formulations of scriptural knowledge. It believes in the direct experience of reality. It aims at drinking the nectar of spiritual life itself instead of getting lost into philosophical reveries of ideas and scriptural knowledge.

Zen is essentially an esoteric practice to attain enlightenment. It aims at freeing the mind from the snares of subjectivity and moralism which forms the basis of all our philosophical and moral notions of good and evil, right and wrong, *Dharma* and *Adharma*. These philosophical and moral notions do not lead to enlightenment. Hui-neg, the sixth Patriarch of Zen Buddhism of China says: "Do not think of good. Do not think of evil. But look at this very moment upon your origins physiognomy, the one which you had even before you were born." Saying so Hui-neg throws light on the essential practical attitude towards life and the world which is to be effectively realized from one instant to another. This pragmatic approach of Zen Buddhism springs from the actual process of inner enlightenment which is called *Satori.* Before entering into meditation and taking vow for either realize the truth or get himself perished. Buddha met many men of learning and scholarship and himself studied the scriptures, but he did not get enlightenment out of the scriptural learning. After scrutinizing and analysing scriptural knowledge he came to the conclusion that the truth can be realized only after experiencing the actual facts of life. He considered suffering, the impermanence of all things and the continual flux of his thought as the only realities on which a philosophical superstructure could be constructed. His inner perception of life and thought process revealed to him the illusion of I-ness and this illusion of his I-ness and his consciousness of so-called self was replaced by the vision of his profound nature of reality. This forced the Buddha to shun metaphysical speculation and to confine himself to the practical means for the elimination of suffering. His philosophy of enlightenment does not encourage scepticism from the fact of life, but to face it directly. Buddha after realizing the truth declared that ignorance is the root of all sufferings. *Nirvāṇa* is the cessation of all sufferings. To get oneself liberated from the wheel of suffering and from the cycle of birth and death it warrants complete attention to the day-to-day fact of life. Inattention is a sin according to Zen-master. The total attention consists of an attitude of non-mental observation of concrete facts arising during day-to-day experience of life. It is living method of approach whose practical character is attached to mind as much as to the matter. Zen Buddhism's pragmatic approach aims at radical transformation of our norms and values by denouncing their contradictions. Zen Buddhism is a method of Science of spiritual delivery which tries to unite and maintain harmony both in the world of inner being and in the world of nature. Robert Linssen rightly observes that as Buddhism is a dialectical pragmatism of psychological and non-mental nature."[11] The Zen Buddhism says that right attention, right vision, right action are the basis of seeing which means to see beyond the body and the familiar peripheral layers of consciousness. It means to penetrate into own's profound essence by means of which one must integrate own-self with the reality. This is Buddha-nature.

Zen Buddhism is totally committed to homogeneity of reality and disappearance of all forms of duality of subject and object. I and the world, *Saṁsāra* and the *Nirvāṇa*. The *Satori* of Zen or the *Nirvāṇa* of *Mahāyāna* Buddhism are nothing other than the realization of homogeneity of the reality. This is the Buddha-nature.

Zen Buddhism is not a religion in the sense commonly used by the Western theologians. It is religion in the sense of uniting and binding and discovering the secret link which bind one to the divine presence which forms the essence of one's own being. In this sense religion may be considered as a science of possible relationship between the human finite and the divine infinite. Thus, Zen Buddhism is based on the philosophy and the religious practice of Tantric mysticism. The mysticism of Zen leads to an effective transcendence of the illusory I-ness. Zen Buddhism has been wrongly understood in the West as refusal of spiritual authority. It is in fact working towards the discovery of an identical nature which is called *tathatā* or *Bodhi-citta*. The *Bodhi-citta* or *tathatā* is the determining factor of harmony, compassion and enlightenment.

The philosophy of Zen Buddhism is based on the concept of absolute freedom. According to Zen Buddhism the essence is freedom. It is enlightenment. It is *Satori*. Any attachment in any form is contrary to freedom. Zen Buddhism says that attachment to any ideas or forms of existence condition the mind and enslave the consciousness. The central reality of our being and of all existence is *tathatā* or *Bodhi-citta*. Any particularization of ideas and values leads to the process of relativity and conditionality. Zen Buddhism is essentially a way of spiritual free thinking and living.

According to Zen Buddhism reality is living truth; pulsation with knowledge and bliss. These are the basic reasons for the sudden, the spontaneous character of enlightenment. We cannot realize infinity by means of time and space which are appearance of reality. We can have the realization of reality only after getting ourselves free from our mental identification with time, space and causality. We cannot discover light by means of darkness which is false of light emanation, therefore, for the attainment of *Satori* we will have to get our mind free from the false value and conditionality which engendered the notion of darkness. This is why all the mystic schools have emphasised that it is impossible to realize the absolute reality by means of I-ness which is false emanation or illusion of the reality.

One of the ill of the technological civilization lies in the technique of the triumph over the various triumphs. Man does not get enough time in modern industrial society to breathe deeply and to live. To maintain the equilibrium of the nervous system has become very important in the modern time where scientism and empty natural rhythms are destroying the inner harmony of life and nature. Modern man is losing his essential nature and reality slowly and gradually in the process of gaining so-called higher form of civilized life. Life is becoming succession of incomplete actions the agitation and restlessness of modern man are depriving him of the natural richness inherent in complete actions. The impatient and the restlessness are the worst enemies of the nerve system and forcing great danger to the preservation of mental health of modern man. The abuse of sexual relation is destroying the higher forms of sensibility. The abnormal increase in the number of insomniacs is one of the worst evils of industrial society. Under these strain and the stress of technical civilization Zen Buddhism's down to earth approach to life is a welcome philosophy. It teaches to conform our life according to the rhythm of nature. The practice of meditation apart from leading to spiritual awakening it has a soothing effect to our nervous system. It is an aid to mental and moral health of the modern man. The deepest laws of our consciousness and certain states akin to *Satori* is revealed during the process of Zen practice of meditation. *Satori* is realizing one's own nature and that nature is not one's own. The practice of Zen Buddhism slowly leads to a new sense of value which supersedes the old one Practice of Zen meditation would result in the birth of a new man who would create a better world and better humanity by harmonizing man with nature. It would destroy all forms of conditionality and relativity. D.T. Suzuki says: "The Buddha was not the mere discoverer of the Twelvefold Chain of Causation, he took the chain in his hands and broke it into pieces, so that it would never again bind him to slavery."[12]

The Zen Buddhism believes in breaking the barriers of conditionality and I-ness so that we can experience *Satori*.

Notes

1. *Dīghanikāya*, Vol. III.
2. *The Archaeology of World Religions* (Jack Finegan) New Jersey, U.S.A.: Princeton University Press, (1965), p. 346.
3. *The Analects of Confucius*, George Allen & Unwin Ltd., London.
4. *The Great Learning & the Mean in Action*, translated by E.R. Hughes, New York: E.P. Dutton & Co. Inc., (1943), p. 111.
5. *Mencius*, translated Lyall, pp. 122, 178.
6. *Science and Civilization in China*, Cambridge University Press, Reprinted, 1977, p. 32.
7. *Zen and Japanese Culture*, pp. 43, 44.
8. *Ibid.*
9. *Ibid.*
10. *Ibid.*, p. 50.
11. *Living Zen*, p. 46.
12. *Essays in Zen Buddhism*, p. 111.

CHAPTER 8
Conclusion

Zen Buddhism has been developed from the teachings of *Laṅkāvatāra Sūtra, Prajñāpāramitā Sūtra, Vajrachedika Sūtra, Avataṁsaka Sūtra,* according to which all beings possess Buddha-nature (*Bodhi-citta*). Buddha-nature is often equated with *tathatā* or *Śūnya,* the realization of which brings about enlightenment. The realization of *tathatā* or *Bodhi-citta* takes man beyond the dualism of subject and object. The reality is *tathatā.* It is called *Śūnya, Bodhi-citta,* suchness and *isness* is *Mahāyāna* tradition. In Chinese, it is called *Chih-mo* or *Shik-mo.* In Japanese the same reality is known as *Kono-mama* or *Sono-mama.* The mystic experience of this state of spiritual sublimity takes a man to the state of *isness* where he is thoroughly purged from all sorts of intellectual and moral considerations. This state of mystic experience cannot be explained through logic and language.

According to this tradition Śākyamuni is the exponent of Zen Buddhism. He passed on the most sacred lesson of Buddhist meditation and esotericism to Venerable Mahākassapa. According to this tradition and believe it is said that Lord Buddha made a mystic declaration that he has transmitted his mystic power in inner spirituality and transcendental meditation to Venerable Mahākassapa which is now known as Zen Buddhism.

According to the other tradition Zen Buddhism as a distinct school of Mahāyāna was born with *Bodhidharma*'s visit to China in 620 A.D. Bodhidharma, according to this tradition, is acknowledged as the first Patriarch and his Chinese disciple *Hui-ko* (468-593) became the second Patriarch of Zen Buddhism.

This form of new Buddhism incorporated in itself the naturalistic mysticism of Taoism and down to earth philosophy of Confucianism. The concept of Buddha-nature and Tao represents the same reality.

Taoism has also incorporated Zen technique to find out the truth. In an endeavour to find out the truth on the other hand, Zen Buddhism is greatly influenced by the Taoist emphasis on natural life. However, Zen Buddhism owes its origin and development from Indian Buddhism. The technique of meditation and the concept of Buddha-nature have definitely been borrowed from the original teachings of Lord Buddha making certain conceptual change and development suited to the creative Chinese mind. The Zen Buddhism came to Japan in seventh century. The Japanese Zen Buddhism owes its development and progress to two great Zen-masters, namely Eisai and Dogen. These two Zen-masters were men of profound spiritual attainment and they transformed Zen into a living religious reality. These two Zen-masters were so great and powerful that they are acclaimed as the founders of the two schools of Zen Buddhism, namely *Rinzai* and *Sōtō*.

These Zen-masters Eisai and Dogen were so much inspired by Zen that they made a pilgrimage to China in search of the authentic and the real form of Zen Buddhism. They visited many monasteries and met many Zen-masters of great spiritual attainments with a purpose of gaining knowledge and testify their own meditations technique and spiritual attainments. *Eisai* after returned from China introduced socio-religious element in his new form of Buddhism which attracted the warrior class of Japan to defend the state against all sorts of invasions and Chiam which was considered as religious duty of this new school. Gradually, it covered the whole gamut of Japanese cultural life. Its impact can be traced in the no play of Japanese poetry *Ikebana* the flower arrangement *Cha-no-va*, tea ceremony etc. all of which emphasise on grace and spontaneity.

Dogen the founder of *Sōtō* school visited *Tendai* monastery of mount *Hiei* in China in search of truth and meaning of life like his teacher *Eisai*. After his returned he introduced a method of meditation known as *Zazen*. He considered the scriptural knowledge and philosophical disputation as an exercise in futility.

Dhyāna is the core-concept of Zen Buddhism. The *nirvāṇa* or *Satori* does not mean to comprehend Buddha-nature in an intellectual or objective sense. It means to become one with it and feel the existence of *tathatā*. in every things and beings. This concepts of *Dhyāna* has been taken from Mahāyāna scriptures such as *Prajñāpāramitā* and *Vīmalakīrtinirdeśa* and *Laṅkāvatāra sūtra*. *Dhyāna* theory of two entrences and four deeds became the basis of its development into different schools of *Mahayana* Buddhism. According to Chinese tradition *Bodhidharma's* long nine years of meditation at the *Shao-Lin-ssu* temple on the mount of *Saung-Shan* during which he neither study any scriptures nor performed any rituals and ceremonies, but kept himself engaged and engrossed in deep meditation proved the efficacy of meditation as the only means of experiencing *satori*. The spirit of this new form of Buddhism in China introduced the practice of Zazen and uphel the importance of sacredness of Chinese family life. Thus, Zen Buddhism integrating the meditational technique of *Bodhidharma* with down to earth philosophical approach of Chinese creative mind became harfinger of a new religious awakening and renaissance.

The characteristic of Zen Buddhism is that it does not give any credence to philosophical abstraction and conceptualization. It lives in facts. The objects of meditation is to integrate the part with the whole, the conscious mind with the unconscious mind and in this process of unification and transfiguration *Satori* is experienced. This process of unification been termed as an art of walking with no path, with no walker and with no goal. This non-sensical statement contains great sense and awareness that though the intellect is a brilliant tool to understand thought and knowledge, but there is something which is beyond the reach of language and thought. This truth of transcendental nature can best be expressed through the language of silence. All the mystical schools like Sufiism, Hindu's *Sahajiyā* cult, and *Upaniṣadic* teachings, Chinese Taoism believe that the supreme reality which forms the basis of all existence and beings, cannot be put into words. It is to be experienced because it is mystical language and reason can lead us to a certain point, but it cannot take us to the core of reality which is called suchness. Intellect, however, serves its purpose by pointing towards the unknown like an arrow mark. This is why the Zen-masters say that if you want to experience *Satori* you should get yourself disassociated with the process of conceptualization and abstraction. The process of *Dhyāna* is a process of freeing the mind from all kinds of dispositions. In Zen Buddhism it is called emptying yourself. There is a famous saying of a Zen-master—"Those who know do not speak—those who speak do not know."

The Buddha's historical silence on fourteen philosophical problems became a matter of great philosophical debate and discussions. Different scholars and Buddhist *Ācāryas* made different interpretations of the Buddha's silence. The Buddha did believe in the reality of *nirvāṇa,* however his silence can only be taken as an inability of the senses and the mind to comprehend it. The philosophical stand taken by the Buddha has some similarity with that of Kant. Kant's use of transcendental dialectic and speculative metaphysics are aimed at exposing the limitation of reason and understanding. He took refuse in faith and practical reason for the realization of transcendental reality because it does not come within the purview of reason and understanding. The Buddha agrees with Kant that reality (*tathatā*) is beyond the reach of reasons and understanding, but he defers from Kant that it is unknown and unknowable. The Buddha is spiritual to the core. *Satori* is to be experienced and lived which is beyond the dualism of subject and object, perfection and imperfection, and finite and infinite.

The observance of the meditational discipline forms the basis of the dawn of *Bodhi-jñāna* (enlightenment). The meditational discipline begets immutability and immutability begets wisdom. There is no other method of self-cultivation. *Suraṅgama-sutta* lists for kinds of purities. It observes that attainment of *nirvāṇa* is not possible without observing the meditational discipline in letter and spirit.

From the early days of the emergence of Zen Buddhism in China there was a practice that an enlightened Zen-master would reside in a little hut often prepared by themselves in a remote mountain side. The seekers after truth used to build-up their own huts nearby to receive direct communication and instructions on different aspects of meditational practice. The seeker used to follow instruction received by the master strictly, student used to seek an audience with the master known as *Zanzen* in a bid to clarify the lessons on *koan* meditation to establish inner rapport with master because it is essential for solving the riddles of *koan*. It is believed that every *koan* has a classical answer. The classical answer is to be discovered by the practitioners; it is considered that the practitioner has perfected the particular *koan* meditation. The whole system of receiving lesson from the Zen-master is the true replica of *Guru-Śiṣya Paramparā* (Teacher-Student Disciple) tradition of Hindu mysticism.

The whole mystic traditions pose a problem that why it is surrounded by esoteric discipline and rules of spiritual conduct? This has provoked the modern so-called scientific mind very much. To find the answer of this problem we shall have to determine the condition and the limits of what is sayable and what is unsayable. The analysis of the logical structure of thought and knowledge have led us to believe that the only those thoughts and knowledge which are rooted in experience alone be given linguistic expression. We cannot deny the existence of transcendental on the basis of our linguistic inability of giving it a linguistic expression. The structure and the function of language have been so designed that it can express what is sayable and it would be better in the word of Wittgenstein to consign to silence what is unsayable. Thus according to Zen Buddhists *Satori* is an experience which can be revealed, felt and lived, but cannot be put into words.

The introduction of *Koan* as meditational technique is to throw the mind of its familiar track of logical reasoning to start the process of emptying it from all sorts of dispositions and metapsychosis. The Zen mystical experience transcends logic and common sense. This is why the transmission of mystical knowledge has been carefully devised through riddles known as a *koan*. In all the mystic traditions there is an universal practice to examine the mental and the moral states of disciple before initiating him into the secret lessons. The philosophical puzzlement and perplexity created in the minds of the disciple by the master paves the path for enlightenment. The very first question of the disciple mirrors the inner crisis and spiritual capability of the disciple. On the careful and the close examination of disciple's mental and moral health Zen-master imparts lessons on different aspects of *koan* and meditation. It is the common practice in Zen tradition to create crisis and restlessness in the disciple's mind only to get out of it successfully. This awakens the inner being and leads him to reality.

Like ancient Indian *Guru* (spiritual teacher) Zen-master also follows the same technique of imparting spiritual instructions which is known as transmission of spiritual power known as *Śakti-pātha*. The role of *Guru* is very important not only in Zen tradition, but in almost all the mystic traditions of the world as he can alone take the disciple after initiation and imparting *koan* lesson to enlightenment. If any person start practising meditation on *koan* without the proper guidance of Master it may lead to disastrous result. It is a moral and spiritual responsibility of every Zen-master to examine the capacity of disciple before imparting lessons on *Koan*, *Zazen* and other forms of meditations. The acclaimed Zen-master has a spiritual power to know the capacity of the disciple for the type and the intensity of meditational practice he deserves to be imparted to a particular person.

The sole objective of Zen meditation is to experience *Satori*. *Satori* is a state of enlightenment. It is spiritual experience which comes after practicing the Zen technique of *koan* and meditation.

An enquiry into the nature of *nirvāṇa* or *Satori* raises another problem that is whether it is attainable in this very life or a person will have to wait till his death. The Buddhist scriptures have thrown enough light on this problem. According to Buddhism there are two kinds of *nirvāṇa*. That is *Sopadiśeṣa* and *Anupadiśeṣa Nibbāṇa Dhātu*. The one means the attainment of *nirvāṇa* makes a man free from all sorts of defilements and delusion but he has to maintain five aggregates to exhaust the *kārmic* energy accumulated in course of cycle of birth and death. The *Anupadiśeṣa Nibbāṇa* means the final liberation from the cycle of birth and death. Zen Buddhism does not enter into this sort of philosophical disputation because it considers that such metaphysical speculation would not lead to *nirvāṇa*. Zen Buddhism takes a very practical view of it and hence its whole emphasis is on the practice of different techniques of meditation so that one can attain the goal, i.e. *nirvāṇa*. According to Zen Buddhism this whole discussion is useless as one state of *nirvāṇa*, inevitably lead to other.

Zen Buddhism is relevant philosophy and way of life for the modern man who is thoroughly disillusioned with modern industrial society and with himself. It has captivated the scientific and the creative mind of Japanese people because it sublimates our thoughts in the splendour of the works of art, literatures and refinement of our mental expressions. For survival and growth of any civilization and humanity sublimation of our baser thoughts into spiritual splendour is necessary. Refinement of our behaviour is *cine quo non*, for the healthy growth and survival of any civilization. Zen Buddhism is both an art and a science which claim to transfigure every individual into Buddha.

The rules of the moral conduct which has been grown under *śīla* (morality), *samādhi* (contemplation) and *paññā* (wisdom) with their assimilation into broader meditational discipline Zen Buddhism promised to create a better world and a better humanity.

The twentieth century world has made many experiments and it has come to the conclusion that neither Marxism nor Western Democracy, neither Existentialism nor Positivism, neither Depth psychology nor Comparative religion could unite the man from himself. To create cohesion and harmony in the society Zen

Buddhism with its lofty philosophy and technique of meditation can integrate the fragmented life of man which is necessary to build-up a better and just society. Zen goes beyond the conceptual teaching of philosophy. It emphasises in integrating the part with the whole and man with humanity. This concept of oneness is the essential part of the Buddha's life and teachings. Zen takes life as a whole. It imparts practical technique to transfigure one's own personality and in this process of transfiguration it fills every single moment of life with grace, spontaneity and significance.

Thus, Zen Buddhism is not an institutionalized religion. It is a way of life. It is way of transformation and transfiguration of human personality. According to Zen Buddhism in each of us there is a Buddha who wants to get himself awakened. Zen Buddhism is nothing but a meditational technique to get our dormant divinity or the Buddha awakened and realized. This is the way through which we can create one world and one humanity.

Bibliography

(A) Primary Sources

Abhinavagupta's *Tantrāloka*, (1921-38). 12 vols., Kashmir Sanskrit Texts and Studies, Vols. 27-39, Srinagar: Kashmir Government Publication.

Aṅguttara-Nikāya (The book of gradual says): Translated by E.M. Hare, Vol. IV, London: Pali Text Society, (1978).

Aṅguttara-Nikāya (The book of gradual says): Translated by F.L. Woodword & Rhys Davids, Vol.V, London: Pali Text Society, (1972).

Avadhūta Gītā, (1954). Kolkata: Dattatreya Avadhuta Ashrama Publication Department, 5 Dehi Entally Road.

Avadhūta Gītā, (2015). Chapt. VIII, verse 1, p. 162, , Chennai: Sri Ramakrishna Math.

Bhāmati, (ed.) Bala Sastri, pp. 1-2.

Bhattacharya, Benayatosh (ed.), (1931). *Guhyasamāja Tantra*, Baroda: Oriental Institute.

Bhattacharya, Benayatosh (ed.), (1952-58). *Sādhanamālā*, 2 Vols., Baroda: Gaekward Oriental Series, XXVI & XLI.

Buddhaghosa, *Bhadantacariya*, (1975). The Path of Purification (*Visuddhimagga*), Translated from the *Pāli* by Bhikkhu Nanamoli. Kandy Srilanka: Buddhist Publication Society. p. 587.

Dhammapada: Translated by Ven. Narada Maha Thera, Colombo, Sri Lanka.

Dīgha-Nikāya (Sinhalese): Sri Lanka: Government Publication.

Kathāvatthu (Points of Controversy): Translated by Shwe Zon Aung and Mrs. Rhys Davids, London: Pali Text Society, (1970).

Kuddhakapāṭha (The minor readings): Translated by Bhikkhu Nyanamoli, London: Pali Text Society, (1978).

Laṅkāvatāra-Sūtra: (Ed. Najio) *Kyoto*, Japan, 1923.

Laṅkāvatāra-Sūtra: translated by D.T. Suzuki, London: Routledge & Kegan Paul, (1959).

Mādhyamikā-kārikā: Nāgārjuna, Ed. L.de La, Vallee, Pussion.

Majjhima-Nikāya (The Collections of Middle Length Sayings): Translated by I.B. Horner, Vols. I, II, III, London: Pali Text Society, (1978, 1975, 1977).

Paratriṁsika.

Patañjali Yoga Sūtra.

Tattvakaumudī, (ed.) Ganganatha Jha, p. 1.

The Buddhacarita or *Life of the Buddha*: *Aśvaghōṣa*, Translated by Edward B. Cowell, New Delhi: Cosmos Publication, (1977).

The Visuddhimagga: *Buddhaghosha*, Ed. C.F. Rhys Davids, The London: Pali Text Society, (1979).

(B) Secondary Sources

Addiss, Stephen and Stanley Lombardo and Judith Roitman (eds.) (2008) *Zen Sourcebook.* Indianpolis: Hackett Publishing Company.

Avalon, Arthur, Ed. (1965). *Kulārṇava Tantra*, (Ganesh & Co., Madras)

Balm, Arehie, *J.* (1958). *Tao Teh* King by Lao Tzu (Frederick Ungar, Publishing Co.), New York.

——, (1977). *The World's Living Religions* (Arnold Heinemann), Delhi

Banerjee, Anukul Chandra (1984). *Aspects of Buddhist Culture from Tibetan Sources*, (Firma KLM Private Limited), Calcutta.

——, (1977). *Studies in Chinese Buddhism* (Firma KLM Private Limited), Calcutta.

Bapat, B.P. (1976). *2500 Years of Buddhism* (Ministry of Information and Broadcasting, Government of India, Fourth Edition).

Bhattacharya, Benayatosh, *An Introduction to Buddhist Esoterism*, Varanasi: Chowkhamba Sanskrit Series.

Bryth, R.H. (1976). *Zen and Zen Classics* (The Roku Seido Press, Vol. III, Fourth Printing), Tokyo, Japan.

Buddhadasa, Bhikkhu (B.E. 2511. *Buddhadhamma for Students* (Śiva Phorn Limited), Bangkok, Thailand.

Burns, Douglas (1968). *Nirvāṇa Nihilism and Satori* (Buddhist Publication Society, Wheel Publication Nos. 117-119), Kandy, Ceylon.

Capra, Fritjof, *The Tao of Physics*.

Carpenter, Edward (1927). *The Art of Creation* (George Allen & Unwin Ltd.), London.

Chan, Wing tsit (1953). *Religious Trends in Modern China* (Columbia University Press), New York.

Change, Chia-Sen (1957). *The Development of Neo-Confucian Thought* (Bookman Association), New York.

Charles, Luch, Lu K'uan Yu (1970). *Ch'an and Zen Teaching* (The clear light series), Berkeley, U.S.A.

Cleary, Thomas (2011). *The Undying Lamp of Zen*. Boston: Shambhala.

Conze, Edward (1975). *Buddhism: Its Essence and Development* (Harper Colophon Books), London.

—— (1962). *Buddhist Thought in India* (George Allen & Unwin Ltd.), London,

Creel, H.G. (1960). *Chinese Thought from Confucius to Mao Tse Tung*. (University of Chicago Press), Chicago.

—— (1949). *Confucius, The Man and the Myth* (John Day & Co.), New York.

Dasgupta, S.B. (1958). *An Introduction to Tantric Buddhism*, University of Calcutta.

Dasgupta, Surendranath (1952). *A History of Indian Philosophy* (Cambridge University Press, Vol. II, London).

Datta, Dhirendra Mohan (1970). *The Chief Current of Contemporary Philosophy* (The University of Calcutta, third Edn.), Calcutta.

Davids, T.W. Rhys (1955). *Buddhist India* [Susil Gupta (India) Limited, Sixth Edition], Calcutta.

Davids, T.W. Rhys (1962). *The History and Literature of Buddhism*. [Susil Gupta (India) Private Ltd., Fourth Edition], Calcutta.

Day, Clarence (1962). *The Philosophers of China*, (Chitadel Press), New York.

Dubb, Homer, H. Hsuntse (1927). *The Moulder of Ancient Confucianism*. (A Probsthain), London.

Dubey, Muchkund (2017). *The Songs of Lalan Shah Fakir*, (Hindi), pp. 78, New Delhi: Sahitya Academic Publication.

Dumoulin, Heinrich. (1988). *Zen Buddhism: A History – India and China*. Blooming, In: *World Wisdom*.

Durant, Will (1993). *Our Oriental Heritage*. New York: MJF Books.

Dutt, Nalinaksha: (1976). *Mahāyāna Buddhism* (Firma KLM Private Limited), Calcutta.

Early Greek Philosophy, p. 108.

Einstein, Albert (2011). *Relativit: The Special and the General Theory*, New Delhi: Mahaveer Publishers.

Eliade, Mircea (1969). *Yoga*, translated from French by Willard R. Trak, (Princeton University Press, Bollingen Series, LVI, Second Edition).

Fang, Thome H. (1967). *The Chinese View of Life* (Union Printing Co.) Kowloon.

Ferguson, Andy (2000). *Zen's Chinese Heritage*, Boston: Wisdom Publications.

Fitzgerald, C.P. (1965). *China: A Short Cultural History* (The Cresset Press, Aylesbury), Benks.

Frost, S.E. (1947). *The Sacred Writings of the World's Great Religions*, (The New Home Library, the Blakinton Company), Philadelphia, U.S.A.

Fung, Yu-Lan (1962). *A Short History of Chinese Philosophy* (The MacMillan Company), New York.

Glimpses of World Religions (1978) (Jaico Publication House, Fifth Impression), Bombay.

Harada, Shodo (2000). *The Path to Bodhi Dharma*. Rutland, Vermont: Tuttle Publishing.

Heisenberg, Werner (1971). *From Physics and Beyond*, Harper & Row.

Heisenberg, Werner (2002). *Physics and Philosophy: The Revolution in Modern Science*. New York: Harper Perennial Modern Thought Publishers.

Hilliard, F.H. (1996). *The Buddha, the Prophet and the Christ* (George Allen & Unwin), London.

Holmes, Edmond (1957). *The Creed of Buddha* (The Bodley Head), London.

Humphreys, Christmas (1981). *Buddhism* (Penguin Books, Reprinted) Great Britain.

——(1959). *Studies in the Middle Way* (George Allen & Unwin Ltd., Third Edition), Great Britain.

——(1969). *The Buddhist Way of Life* (Unwin Books, George Allen & Unwin Ltd.) London, U.K.

——(1962). *Zen: A Way of Life* (The English University Press), London, U.K.

——(1961). *Zen Buddhism* (Unwin Books) London, U.K.

——(1960). *Zen Comes West* (George Allen & Unwin Ltd.), London, U.K.

Juniper, Andrew, (2003). *Wabi Sabi the Japanese Art of Impermanence*, p. 159, Tokyo: TUTTLE Publishing.

Kalpeau, Philip (1972). *The Three Pillars of Zen* (Beacon Press, 9th Edition) Boston, U.S.A.

——(1979). *Zen Dawn in the West* (Anchor Press), New York.

Kalupahana, David J. (1977). *Buddhist Philosophy* (The University Press of Hawaii, Second Edition), Honolulu.

Kapleau, Philip (1965). *The Three Pillars of Zen*. New York: Anchor Books.

Kaviraj, Gopinath (Ed.): *Yoginī Hṛdaya* (Saraswati Granthmala), Varanasi.

Konneth, Rōshi, Jiju (1976). *Zen the Eternal Life* (Dhamma Publishing), California, U.S.A.

Kraft, Kenneth (ed.) (1988). *Zen: Tradition and Transition*. New York: Groove/Atlantic.

Kraft, Kenneth (ed.) (2000). *Zen Teaching, Zen Practice*. Boston: Weatherhill.

Kularatne, H. de. S. *The Essence of Buddha-Dharma* (The South Ceylon Youth Council Printing Section), Galle, Ceylon.

Lineseen, Robert (1958). *Living Zen* (Translated by Diana Abrahams Curiel-George Allen & Unwin Ltd., English Edition first published) U.K.

Ling, Trevor 1973. *The Buddha* (Temple Smith), London.

Ling, Yutang (1959). *My Country and My People* (John Day & Co.), New York.

Li-Tsun-Hsin (1929). *Transmission of the Lamp.*

Liu-Wu-Chi (1955). *A Short History of Confucian Philosophy* (Penguin Book Ltd.), Harmondsworth.

Marshall, Sir John (1931). *Mahenjodaro and the Indus Valley Civilization*, 41, Great Russell Street, London.

Max Kaltenmark (1969). *Lao Tzu and Taoism*, Translated by the French; by Roger Greaves. Stanford, California: Stanford University Press. p. 52.

McDaniel, Richard Bryan (2012). *Zen Masters of China: The First Step East.* Rutland, VT: Tuttle Publishing.

McDaniel, Richard Bryan (2012). *Zen Masters of Japan: The First Step East.* Rutland, VT: Tuttle Publishing.

Mei, Y.P. Mobe (1934). *The Neglected Rival of Confucius* (A. Probsthain), London.

Mencius, Translated Lyall, pp. 122, 178.

Mendis, N.K.G. (1985). *The Abhidhamma in Practice* (Buddhist Publication Society Wheel Publication Nos. 322-323) Kandy, Sri Lanka.

Mercia Eliade (1958). *Yoga Immortality and Freedom*, Translated by the French Willard R. Trask. Bollingen Foundation Inc.

Mostow, Alexander (1961). *A Study in Wittgenstain's Tractatus* (University of California) U.S.A.

Müller, F. Max (1974). *The Sacred Books of the East* (Motilal Banarasidass) Delhi.

Murti, T.R.V., *The Central Philosophy of Buddhism*, pp. 142-143.

Narada, Maha Thera (1968). *A Manual of Abhidhamma* (Buddhist Publication Society), Kandy, Ceylon.

Narasu, P. Laksmi (1964). *What is Buddhism* (Maha Bodhi Society, Third Edition), Calcutta.

Needham, Joseph (1977). *Science and Civilization in China* (Cambridge University Press, Vol. II), London.

Nigosian, S.A. (1974). *World Religions* (Adward Arnold), London.

Okakuro-Kakuzo, *The Book of Tea*, New York: Fox Duffield.

Pande, G.C. (1993). *Studies in Mahayana*, Saranath, Varanasi: Central Institute of Higher Tibetan Studies.

Pandit, M.P. (1959). *Kuṇḍalanī Yoga* (Ganesh & Co.), Madras.

Philosophy of Gorakhnath, p. 172. Gorakhpur: Mahant Digvijay Nath Trust, Gorakhnath Temple.

Pitcher, George (1964). *The Philosophy of Wittgenstein* (Prentice-Hall of India Private Limited, New Delhi).

Piyadassi, Thera (1979). *The Buddha's Ancient Path* (Buddhist Publication Society), Kandy, Sri Lanka.

Radhakrishnan, S. (1977). *Indian Philosophy* (George Allen & Unwin Ltd., Vol.I, Tenth Impression, London).

Rahula, Walpola (1978). *Zen and the Taming of the Bulk* (Gordon Fraser) London.

——(1978). *What the Buddha Taught* (Gordon Fraser, Unwin Brothers Ltd.), Great Britain.

Randall, Lisa (2011). *Knocking on Heaven's Door*. New York: Harper Collins Publisher.

Reps, Paul (1959). *Zen Fleash, Zen Bones* (Charles R. Tuttle Co.), Tokyo, Japan.

Reps, Paul and Nyogen Senzaki (1998). *Zen Flesh, Zen Bones*. Rutland, VT.: Tuttle Publishing.

Robert, Aitkin (1982). *Taking the Path of Zen*. New York: North Point Press.

Robinson, Richard, H. (1976). *Early Madhyamika in India and China* (Motilal Banarasidass), Delhi.

Ryokan (2006). *One Robe, One Bowl: The Zen Poetry of Ryokan*. Boston: Weatherhill.

Sasaki, Ruths, Fuller (1960). *Rinsai Zen Study for Foreigners in Japan* (The Nissha Printing Co. Ltd.), Japan.

——(1953). *The Development of Chinese Zen* (The First Zen Institute of America Inc.), New York.

——(1959). *Zen a Method of Religious Awakening*, Nissha Printing Co. Ltd., Kyoto, Japan.

Schlaeg I. Irmgard (1975). *The Wisdom of the Zen-masters* (Sheldom Press), London.

Schrödinger, Ervin (1983). *My Views of the World*, Connecticut: Ox Bow Press, Woodbridge.

Schrödinger, Erwin (1952). *Nature and the Greeks*, Cambridge University Press.

Schrödinger, Erwin (1952). *Science and Humanism*, Cambridge University Press.

Schrödinger, Erwin (1952). *Science and Humanism, Physics in our Times* Cambridge University Press.

Sekida, Katsuki (2005). *Two Zen Classics*. Boston: Shambala.

Singh, Jaidev (1979). *Śiva Sūtra*. The Yoga of Supreme Identity, Delhi: Motilal Banarasidass Publishers Pvt. Ltd.

Singh, L.P. (1976). *Tantra: Its Mystic and Scientific Basis* (Concept Publishing Company), New Delhi.

Singh, Lalan Prasad (2010). *Buddhist Tantra: A Philosophical Reflection and Religious Investigation*, New Delhi: Concept Publishing Company Pvt. Ltd.

Singh, Lalan Prasad (2010). *Tantra: It's Mystic and Scientific Basis*. New Delhi: Concept Publication Company Pvt. Ltd.

Singh, Lalan Prasad (2016). *Science, Spirituality and Ontological Mysticism,* New Delhi: Concept Publishing Co. Pvt. Ltd.

Sircar, Mahendranath (1974). *Hindu Mysticism* (Oriental Books Reprint Corporation), New York.

Steberbatsky, Theo (1975). *The Conception of Buddhist Nirvāṇa* (Bharatiya Vidya Prakashan, Second Edition), Delhi.

Suzuki, Beatrice Lane (1959). *Mahayana Buddhism* (George Allen & Unwin Ltd.), London.

Suzuki, D.T. (1958). *Essays in Zen Buddhism* (Rider & Company, Vols. I, II, III), London.

——(1957). *Studies in the Laṅkāvatāra-Sūtra* (Routledge & Kegan Paul Ltd., Reprinted), London.

——(1957). *Studies in Zen* (Published for Buddhist Society, London, by Rider-London, Second Impression).

——(1959). *The Training of the Zen Buddhist Monk* (University Books), New York, U.S.A.

——(1959). *Zen and Japanese Culture* (Routledge & Kegan Paul Ltd.), London.

Suzuki, D.T. (1991). *The Zen Doctrine of No-Mind.* Newburyport, MA: Samuel Weiser.

Suzuki, D.T. (1994). *Essays in Zen Buddhism,* First Series. New York: Grove Press.

Suzuki, D.T. (2010). *Zen and Japanese Culture.* Princeton University Press.

Suzuki, D.T., *On Indian Mahayana Buddhism,* p. 122.

Swann, Jeffrey (1962). *Teohold on Zen* (Ruskin House, George Allen & Unwin Ltd.), London.

The Analects of Confucius (George Allen & Unwin Ltd.), London.

The Essentials of Tao, Tao Te Ching, Translated and presented by Thomas Cleary, 1993, Herper San Francisco, Verse 56.

The Great Learning and the Mean-in-Action (Translated by E.R. Hughes, E.P. Dutton & Company Inc., New York, (1943, p. 111).

Thien, An, Thich (1975). *Zen Philosophy Zen Practice* (Dhamma Publishing) U.S.A.

Tractatus Logico-Philosophicus, Wittgenstein, Routledge Taylor & Francis Group.

Underhill, Evelyn (1960). *Mysticism,* Methuen & Co. Ltd., 36, Essex Street Strand, London: University Paperbacks.

Wach, Joachim (1958). *The Comparative of Religious* (Morningside Heights, Columbia University Press), New York, U.S.A.

Waddell, Norman (1984). *The Unborn: The Life and Teachings of Zen Master Bankei.* New York: North Point Press.

Ware, James, R. (1955). *The Savings of Confucius* (New American Library), New York.

Washington Post, 25th September, 2011. *Faster than Light*: *Revolution or Error*. Particles Burst Einstein's Speed Limit by Brian Vastag.

Watts, Alan (1999). *The Way of Zen*. New York: Vintage.

Watts, Allan W. (1958). *The Way of Zen* (Pantheon Third Printing), New York, U.S.A.

Webber, Max (1951). *The Religion of China* (Confucianism and Taoism) Translated and Edited by Hons H. Gerth, (The Free Press, Glencoe), Illinois, U.S.A.

Wei, Wu Wei (1963). *Ask the Awakened* (Routledge & Kegan Paul), London.

Wettamuny, R.G.de.S.: *Buddhism and Its Relation to Religion and Science* (M.D. Gunasena & Co. Ltd.).

Wright, Arthur, F. (1959). *Buddhism in Chinese History*, (Oxford University Press).

Zimmer, Heinrich (1960). *Philosophies of India* (Compbell, Meridi & Books, Ed. by Joseph), New York, U.S.A.

(C) Encyclopaedias

Encyclopaedia of Buddhism, Vol. III, by G.P. Malalasekera, 1972, Published by the Government of Sri Lanka, Ceylon: Government Press, p. 194.

International Encyclopaedia of the Social Sciences (1972) (The MacMillan Company & The Free Press, Vol. I, Reprint Edition), New York, U.S.A.

Malalasekara, G.P. (1972). *The Encyclopaedia of Buddhism* (Government Press, Government of Ceylon, Vol. III), Ceylon.

The Encyclopaedia of Religion and Ethics (Hastings, James; Charles Scribner's Sons Mission and Gibb Limited, Vols. IV, VII & XI), New York, U.S.S.

The New Encyclopaedia Britannica (1975) (Encyclopaedia Britannica Inc., Vols. III & V, 15th Edition) U.S.A.

The New Encyclopaedia Britannica, Vol. 3, by Encyclopeadia Britannica Inc. 1976, U.S.A., p. 386.

(D) Dictionaries

Buddhadatta, A.P. (1979). *English-Pali Dictionary* (The Text Society, Reprinted), London.

Davids, T.W. and William Steds (1972). *The Pali Text Society's Pali-English Dictionary* (The Pali Text Society), London, U.K.

Malalasekara, G.P. (1974). *Dictionary or Pali-Proper Names* (The Pali Text Society, Reprinted, Vol. II), London, U.K.

Nyanatiloka: *Buddhist Dictionary* (1980). (Buddhist Publication Society), Kandy, Sri Lanka.

(E) Journals

Dhyāna in Early Buddhism, Indian Historical Quarterly, III, (1927).
Journal of the Pāli Text Society, The London: Pali Text Society, , Vol. V, (1981).
Mind, A Quarterly Review of Psychology and Philosophy, Vol. 21, 1912, Kraus, Reprinted Limited, Edited by Prof. G.F. Stout (Leone, H.), West Germany.
Nirvāṇa Nihilism and Satori, Buddhist Publication Society (by Douglas, M. Burns) The Wheel Publication Nos. 117-119, Kandy, Ceylon.
The Mahā Bodhi, A Monthly Journal, Vol. 69, Number 5, Calcutta, 1961.
The Mahā Bodhi, International Buddhist Monthly, Vol. 64, Calcutta, May 1956.
The Times of India, Editorial, Monday, May 26, 1986, p. 6.
The Times of India, Sunday Review (by Ram Swarup), Sunday, August 1986.

Index